T0345123

# Inspiring Remote Tech Teams

# Inspiring Remote Tech Teams

## Keys to Leadership and Purposeful Performance

**Hubbert Smith**

CRC Press
Taylor & Francis Group
Boca Raton London New York

CRC Press is an imprint of the
Taylor & Francis Group, an **informa** business
AN AUERBACH BOOK

CRC Press
Taylor & Francis Group
6000 Broken Sound Parkway NW, Suite 300
Boca Raton, FL 33487-2742

© 2021 by Hubbert Smith

CRC Press is an imprint of Taylor & Francis Group, an Informa business

No claim to original U.S. Government works

Printed on acid-free paper

International Standard Book Number-13:
978-0-367-76922-2 (Hardback)
978-0-367-64475-8 (Paperback)
978-1-003-12469-6 (eBook)

**Visit the Taylor & Francis Web site at**
**http://www.taylorandfrancis.com**

**and the CRC Press Web site at**
**http://www.crcpress.com**

## Trademarks Used in This Book

# Dedication

To my wife Vicki, an inspiration to us all.
To our awesome children—Thomas, Hannah, Sasha, and Leah.
Readers, please vote for them when they run for President.

# Contents

# List of Illustrations

## List of Figures

## List of Tables

# Foreword

**Thomas DiGiacomo**
**President of Engineering and Innovation at SUSE**

When Hubbert shared his idea to write about effective remote teams, I certainly thought the topic deserved high attention, especially during and post 2020. But I questioned if we (actually, if I, especially) could really benefit from another deep look at this essential topic.

Having led large, globally distributed remote teams for many years, I understand how to make teamwork happen in an effective way, especially within the open source world in which people are contributing code and collaborating with each other from wherever they are. Despite everyone being remote, on different time zones, using different languages, and having very diverse cultures, this has worked well for open source, enabling the most important software and innovations of our times, I would dare to say.

As much as I knew how to efficiently set up remote teams, Hubbert's vision and examples opened my eyes to the fact that there is even more to it than my years of experience and expertise have provided.

Connecting the neuroscience and human aspects opened my eyes to the approaches we apply to bringing remote teams together, to increasing belonging, and to creating nurturing "communities." Remote teams in 2020 look very different from those in prior years and will continue to evolve in future. In 2019, even teams who were remote were able to travel and meet when needed, without today's concerns of family health, safety, education, or the greater responsibilities to care for family while working from home. Our evolved version of remote tech teams is vastly different and needs to be considered as such.

Community is not a substanceless, random word for projects and contributors. Community reflects our need to work on common goals and be with each other on such a journey.

So, for me and other tech people, leaders, and members of remote teams, we will be awakened by all the fantastic hands-on hints, best practices, and guiding principles based on solid ground that Hubbert provides in *Inspiring Remote Tech Teams*. We will be better prepared and better equipped to both contribute and lead efficiently in the digital economies that shape the future of our world.

# Preface

*Inspiring Remote Tech Teams* is a trail map to building effective teams and organizations—now, as world health dictates remote work, and in the future, as global talent pools contribute to our digital economy.

Humans are wired to be social, and world events require social distancing from our office community. The absence of "community" triggers primitive brain responses. These instinctual responses of survival, social belonging, and the power of story all profoundly surface during our reaction as we adjust to remote work.

This trail map for team leaders improves team execution despite physical separation. The book covers simple neuroscience as it applies to our "separation." It is a hands-on guide to maintaining and improving teamwork working remotely. We can create a positive sense of enthusiasm, engagement, and contribution even when working apart. It is also a hands-on guide at the intersection of teams + remote + laymen's neuroscience to create a positive sense of enthusiasm, engagement, and contribution, even when working apart.

This book is different from most others:

- Remote teams, now and for the future, are the pathway to using global talent effectively.
- We examine the combination of the "hard skills" of tech team project management and the "soft skills" of healthy distributed teams: remote offices, sales offices, partners, suppliers, customers, and teams engaging global talent pools.
- We all carry primitive instinct and emotion from thousands of generations. This is a fact. Despite the ongoing evolution and advancement of our brains, these instincts remain. Our primitive instincts and emotions can be either

negative or positive for teams. We must consciously adjust our leadership and our workplaces to compensate for the magnified instincts and emotions caused by the absence of community (tribe).

- A study of laymen's neuroscience clarifies what does, or does not, work well in teams. Laymen's neuroscience helps us understand "why." The practical examples and best practices offer hands-on methods to use our neuroscience to help teams be their best, to improve collaboration, and to deliver consistent team results.

— Hubbert Smith
October 22, 2020

# Acknowledgments

Thanks sincerely to John Wyzalek of Taylor & Francis and Theron R. Shreve and Susan Culligan of DerryField Publishing Services. Their contributions have made this a better book.

# About the Author

Hubbert Smith has had a 30+-year career in tech. He's led 26 successful projects for business leaders including Samsung, Intel, and WD. He is a published author, a patent holder, and currently the VP of Customer Success at Geminos.AI.

World events have magnified remote work. Remote work is the new norm. Successful organizations are good at teamwork; it takes leadership, discipline and practice. Effective remote team work with a global talent pool is a force multiplier for organizational success. Zoom alone does not make an effective team.

# Chapter 1

# Our Wiring and Our People

This section introduces workplace neuroscience. Specifically, the brain chemistry associated with your instincts can be your best asset to achieve effective teams and tap into global talent—or workplace neuroscience be the worst enemy of effective teams.

## 1.1 Everyone Needs a Place, Everyone Needs a Purpose

We all have primitive instincts. These primitive social instincts come into play with remote teams. Sometimes remote teams work, and sometimes remote teams fail spectacularly. This book explores remote teams, the impact of our primitive wiring, and actionable suggestions on how to make the best of our new remote workplace reality, to become a standout leader.

Our instinctive wiring is further challenged by remote teams. Being away from the office takes away our "place," takes away our "community." When we are isolated, we feel loss. We may feel the loss of our place, and we may feel we have lost our purpose.

Creating effective remote teams starts with our most elementary needs as humans. These fundamental needs are better understood with insights provided by basic neuroscience.

It is not my intention to teach you the various parts of the brain and anatomical responses. Although this may be interesting, it would be mostly irrelevant for remote teams. Rather, the mission is to offer a practical trail map for effective remote teams, and neuroscience and psychology are referenced to better understand "why" people are the way they are in teams and what to do about it.

It takes attention to create that healthy "place" in which people feel they belong. The way to prime the pump is to work together on shared goals, place a priority on helping each other achieve our parts of the shared goals, and help each other longer term with career mentoring. Everyone can be a mentor in some form or fashion.

Mentoring creates tangible benefits to everyone. Trust, respect, belonging, friendship, are developed just by the simple and repeated act of helping others learn. Mentoring is its own reward to mentors, to the team lead, to the employer, and of course to the person learning and being mentored. To create a healthy team, encourage mentoring and learning. More on this later in the book.

## 1.2 Our Primitive, and Fearful, Wiring

Seventy thousand years ago, humans used gestures, expressions, and primitive language to communicate.

- The *tiger* is in the west (*negative* stimuli, *immediate*)
- The edible *berries* are in the west (*positive* stimuli, can be *deferred*)

After a bit of trial and error (aka, evolution), our primitive human wiring caused us to magnify and listen to the immediate negative stimuli and stay away from the tiger, ignoring the feel-good food stimuli. Our primitive wiring comes into play in these modern times. When we feel alone, our primitive instinct kicks in. When we feel threatened, our survival instinct kicks in. And neuroscience shows clearly that primitive stimuli causes primitive parts of our brains to override the advanced frontal lobe brain activity—we literally stop thinking logically when presented with primitive stimuli.

Our primitive reactions to stimuli apply to remote teams today. In most work scenarios, it takes teams of people to accomplish anything of significance. Teams fail, and projects fail, with alarmingly high frequency. Virtual, remote workplaces, social distancing, contract workers, experts, partners, work-from-home, and 100 percent remote organizations are with us now and into the future. Remote teams are more than a simple convenience—remote teams are a necessity driven by global competition.

Primitive stimuli are at play in today's modern remote/virtual workplaces. We are more alone as a result of the ability to work from home, virtual teams, and 100 percent distributed businesses. Sociologists note that our societies have ever-increasing stress levels.

Why is that? It is reasonable to connect the dots between our primitive wiring to survive and belong, to our perceived "loss of community." We once had a community of coworkers and cohorts when we went to the office; now we experience the absence of that community caused by social distancing and remote workplaces.

We, as leaders, can avoid pushing all those "negative" buttons in our primitive wiring. We can easily avoid "survival" responses. We can instead push the "positive" buttons to restore our sense of "community." Push the buttons to stimulate anticipation, focus, learning, and the desire to be successful. When we apply the right stimulus, we improve both job satisfaction and the results of remote teams.

---

**GOOD PRACTICES**

» Before any meeting or conversation, think through your words carefully.
» Make a conscious effort to avoid survival wiring, which diminishes our ability to think logically. If there is a problem, say, "We are challenged to find a solution," rather than using negatively burdened phrases or placing blame.
» Make a conscious effort to build belonging and community. When there is a success, say, "We did this together": the team gets the credit. Emphasize team results (not individual results).

---

 This is my "place." This is my "purpose." I am part of something important and bigger than myself. I anticipate team success. I participate, my contributions are valued. I am safe.

## 1.2.1 Surviving → Belonging → Becoming

Our instincts are strong: → **Surviving** → **Belonging** → **Becoming** is so obvious.

- *Surviving* is foundational and immediate, processed by the most primitive parts of our brains. When our neurological survival response kicks in, other higher-order parts of our brains, such as those controlling reason and logic, are shut down. Survival thinking overrides all other thinking.
- *Belonging.* Community wiring happens in those slightly more advanced parts of our brains that control emotion. Our instinct to belong is bit less immediate but is nonetheless foundational. Our instincts tell us that our chances of survival and reproduction are significantly increased within a community. And our behavior, bearing, and emotions vary depending on whether or not we are with our community. Processing basic emotions such as fear, reasoning, creativity, and physical capabilities are altered if we are (or are not) with our community. Ever notice why we powerfully respond to a good story, why we cannot put down a good book, why we cry at movies? This is "group belonging" wiring, and it overrides other higher-order thinking—other, that is, than our survival instinct.

- **Becoming.** Our ambitions driving our need to learn, achieve mastery, security, reputation, status, wealth, and the like are processed by the most developed part of our brains, the frontal lobe. We are able to use these most developed areas of our brain to think logically—but only if survival or primitive wiring doesn't get in the way. Keeping our thoughts in the higher order of logic and reason is also known as *emotional intelligence,* meaning we consciously overcome our lizard brains and think with logic and reason, even when our lizard brains are grabbing for the steering wheel.

### 1.2.2 Instinct

Instinct is something *we just know.* Merriam-Webster defines instinct as *a behavior mediated by reactions below the conscious level.* Instinct is not consciously learned. Instinct is below the conscious level. We know how to breathe, eat, and drink. We know how to use our hands and feet. For 80,000 years of human evolution, for 4,000 generations, our instincts have evolved and been strengthened. Then modern society happened, and the modern workplace happened. And our instincts have not kept pace with these dramatic changes in the nature of our existence.

- Our instincts are not going to change.
- Modern society isn't going away.
- The modern workplace isn't going away.

Our path will either conveniently ignore our surviving-belonging-becoming instincts, *or,* our path will embrace these instincts as an asset, as a strength. But developing any strength, we must *decide* to apply the consistent effort and consistent practice to develop strengths into skills, into tangible reward.

### 1.2.3 Maslow's Pyramid and Surviving[1]

Maslow's pyramid of self-fulfillment (see Figure 1.1) shows that our most basic need is survival: physical survival, physical safety—don't get eaten; don't get killed for your stuff; have food, drink, and shelter.

This surviving is handled by your "lizard brain" (the scientific name is the *amygdala*). The amygdala processes the most foundational and basic survival emotions: anger, fear, sex.

---

[1] Maslow, A. H. (1943). Conflict, frustration, and the theory of threat. *The Journal of Abnormal and Social Psychology,* 38(1); Maslow, A. H., Frager, R., Fadiman, J., McReynolds, C., & Cox, R. (1954). *Motivation and Personality.* New York: Pearson.

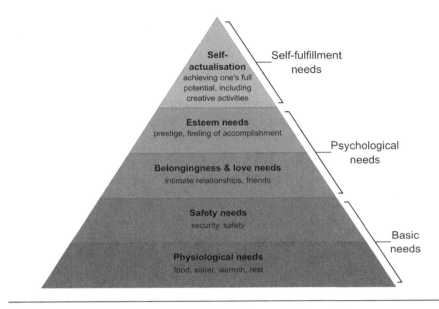

**Figure 1.1** Maslow's Hierarchy of Needs (*Source:* Wikipedia)

When our survival emotion is stimulated, the amygdala shouts out the other, more advanced portions of our brains. We literally lose the ability to think logically when our survival is threatened, or perceived to be threatened, as regrettably happens so often with exaggerations by the media.

When we hear bad news, our amygdala drowns out thoughts from other parts of the brain, such as our ability to reason. In business literature, we hear the concept of *emotional quotient* (EQ); this is our ability to quiet survival responses, which allow other, higher-order brain functions such as reasoning to be heard.

*So, what do we do with this information?* We team leaders and teammates should (and can) avoid workplace conflict which makes our survival response kick in. Instead, we should (and can) work toward workplace conditions that make our belonging and becoming instincts kick in.

Following is just one example of how our brain wiring impacts business, and what to do about it:

## Acquisitions

Acquisitions are commonplace, and when acquisitions fail, businesses and employees are deeply impacted, and job satisfaction and perceived job security are drastically diminished. Threats to job security trigger the survival instinct. We are more inclined to make snap judgments than to think logically. We certainly don't do our best work with our amygdala shouting at us to run away.

Tech companies are acquired all the time. Acquisition is just another type of project, typically with a large tech component, and typically involving remote participants.

On both sides of the table, our primitive wiring immediately kicks in: it's *us* vs. *them*. Our inner dialog in our primitive minds repeats, "Will I survive or will I not?" (This inner dialog plays in everyone's mind.)

Q: What do we do about it?
A: We are all wired with the need for a purpose. We are all wired with the need for a place.

Team leaders can create that purpose by starting with clear goals to paint the picture of success. Team leaders can create that place starting with a one-to-one conversations with team members to establish personal communication, setting everyone up for success.

Acquisitions fail all the time, a fact that we will cover in more detail later in this book.

## Maslow's Pyramid and Belonging

We all need a place. We have a deeply held need to belong, to be social, to have relationships, to belong to a group, family, religion, town, or guild. We are wired to find a place within our community. Our instincts form a need to both get and give love, affection, and friendship. This is worth repeating: we have an instinct to belong. This is not something learned or imitated; we come into the world with this inherent need. Relationships matter. Acceptance matters.

*So, what do we do with this information?* We team leaders and teammates should (and can) treat each other with value and respect. We can be gentle with our criticism. We can be generous with our recognition of contribution. We can embrace our shared experiences with the rough edges. And we can avoid workplace problems that make our survival response kick in.

## Maslow's Pyramid and Becoming

We all need a purpose; we are deeply wired to learn, grow, achieve. We are wired to find a feeling of value, to find respect, and to find self-esteem. This is more than just belonging to a group. The instinct to "become" drives us to seek our purpose—to seek recognition, freedom, independence, and wealth. At a deeper personal level, our need to become drives us to seek completeness, to have empathy, to help others—and gives us the ability to know joy.

*So, what do we do with this information?* We team leaders and teammates should (and can) treat each other with value and respect. We are all imperfectly striving, and we can collaborate to find our shared purpose and our individual purposes. This is worth repeating: we can embrace our shared experiences with all the rough edges. And we can avoid workplace animus that makes our survival response kick in.

## 1.3 Dopamine and Story

Dopamine[2,3,4] (aka, the messenger of the brain) is a hormone that functions as a neurotransmitter. When stimulated, nerve cells release dopamine, and this release sends (happy) signals to other nerve cells.

Dopamine is triggered as our advance reward for seeking and learning. Pavlov's dog heard the bell and anticipated the food.[5] This experiment proved the stimuli of *predicted* rewards, anticipation. The significance of Pavlov's experiment is that it proves the system of reward-for-learning in the brain. Now, it is easy to imagine a dog in the wild who senses prey, anticipates eating—and whose brain releases dopamine, which rewards the dog immediately for hunting down the prey. In humans, dopamine is much the same. It is a type of incentive system for the approach of a reward—the anticipation of a good meal, a good book, a lover, and the like.

Dopamine is part of our becoming wiring related to motivation and ambition. Dopamine influences our *motivational* behavior. Dopamine motivates us toward or away from an outcome. The relevance in the workplace is obvious. Dopamine effects mood, attention, feelings of wellbeing, learning, motor control, and muscle memory.

Ever wonder why playing or listening to music makes your brain feel good? Your brain likes the patterns, your brain likes the repeating melodies, the repeating arpeggios, chord tension, and resolution. Dopamine is at work when your brain anticipates the next passage. Our minds are chemically rewarded by dopamine as we process music.

Ever wonder why we like music with lyrics that tell a story? Again, our dopamine levels are increased by anticipating the tension and resolution of the story, in addition to the musical anticipation. The popularity of music videos is no

2   WebMD: https://www.webmd.com/mental-health/what-is-dopamine#1

3   *Psychology Today:* https://www.psychologytoday.com/us/basics/dopamine

4   *Neuroscience News:* https://neurosciencenews.com/dopamine-learning-reward-3157/

5   https://www.britannica.com/science/Pavlovian-conditioning

surprise, as it combines the anticipation of *visual* tension/resolution to *musical* tension/resolution and *spoken lyrics* tension/resolution.

This matters to remote tech teams when the team hears the story, embraces the story, sees themselves as participants in the story. Our buy-in and anticipation is rewarded by dopamine. This is positive influence for remote tech projects. Conversely, the buy-in and dopamine response can be turned to ashes with a poorly communicated or constantly changing story. Project change is exhausting, first because wasteful revisions could have been easily avoided; second because when the project story is erased, our mental picture of success, our mental picture of ourselves as participants, are all erased. The buy-in and dopamine response is erased.

Thankfully, there are methods to control project change, to keep that clear mental picture unchanging, front and center. And these methods are covered in this book.

Dopamine levels are drastically reduced by poor sleep and are boosted by exercise, sleep, and daily exercise. And so when we feel unmotivated, joyless, less than 100 percent, it is likely due to the lack of sleep, good diet, and meaningful motivation, with the resulting deficiency of dopamine.

When you feel apathy about working or about a new project, visualize the completed work, and the power of "story" kicks in. Story paints the picture of reward, nudging our brains to anticipate the reward of a completed project—and our brains right then and there produce (happy) dopamine, which improves our focus, mood, motivation, and ambition.

### 1.3.1 Our Primitive Wiring for Story

Telling a clear and compelling story of our shared successful project is both appropriate and effective. You can paint the big picture and put in all the small details, including how each team member plays an indispensable role. This project story creates a sense of purpose, creates a sense of "community," and is a highly effective way to generate engagement, trust, and results. This is where our brain chemistry is a giant asset. We learn by story. In our mind's eye we see the story, we see our place in the story, and, based on significant research, these mental images are processed by our brain just like reality.

This task of the team leader increases in relevance for remote teams, where that consistent, clear, shared vision isn't carried by face-to-face meetings. The team leader should (and absolutely can) improve team effectiveness by clear and consistent pictures of the project, each team member's role, the many small challenges that will be faced and overcome, and how we will deliver results. It's the details of a good book or movie that make them captivating. And so, as you tell the story of your project, include how you will overcome those rough edges, those obstacles and setbacks.

## 1.3.2 Story and Remote Teams

If it's a project or if it's an operations function, every team needs a clear picture of success. This book dwells on projects, but it's all applicable to any remote team.

Build the mental image of the project journey, project results success, and key success metrics, including the rough parts. Our brains are wired for stories; telling the project story stimulates our brains to create mental engagement, just as with a good book or a good movie.

- Telling the "project story" creates a connection with the team.
- Story leaves the team with a stronger and well-remembered mental picture of success and their role in success.
- Story focuses a feeling of belonging, contributing to something larger, improving morale and results.
- Story shows individuals their part in the bigger picture.
- Story gives teams a shared understanding. Story makes it easier to safely speak up and contribute, and constructive feedback is interpreted only as feedback, not an attack.
- Story creates safety, which leads to improved morale and results.
- So, team leader, "tell the story" and find your community.

*Assume the positive.* Assuming the positive means we assume people are generally self-motivating, are hardworking, take pride in the quality of their work, and willingly work with teammates.

## 1.3.3 "Painting the Picture" with Common Goals

Teams click when all members clearly visualize the finish line (the success criteria) and claim victory. "We know the goals. Now let's be a community and work together." That consistent picture of success should not change.

If a team leader sets clear goals and the measurable success criteria early, providing reasonable resources and reasonable time to do the job or project, there is every reason to believe the job or project will be a success, 100% of the time.

Why do projects fail? Why do teams fail? Why do remote teams fail (a lot)?

Projects don't fail because of individuals. Projects fail because of poorly conceived or changing requirements coupled with penny pinching and inadequate resources.

- **Scope.** Lack of clear goals, constantly changing goals, unclear or unrealistic quality expectations, missing (forgetting, ignoring) big pieces, such as sales, training, end user success management, support, pricing, competition.
- **Schedule.** Inadequate or unrealistic schedule expectations. Long schedules during which needs or competition changes make the project irrelevant.
- **Resources.** Lack of the right resources, skills, personnel; ongoing resource erosion.
- **Poor execution,** leading to schedule slips.

When projects fail, the root causes can most often be traced to management team's changing scope, or success criteria, and/or penny pinching. This translates to a mental picture of inconsistent and unreachable objectives. We want to avoid failure, survival responses kick in, which then diminishes the functioning of our frontal lobe and our drive to belong and become. And when we are remote, without our community, the survival response is magnified.

It is no surprise that the remedy to better engage our desire to belong and become is to keep the picture of success clear and consistent, keep resources clear and consistent, and not move the finish line.

## 1.3.4 Story and Credibility

Story works when we can visualize ourselves in our mind's eye without doubt or distortion of the truth.

If our mental picture is believable, this mental view begins to become our view of reality. Our memories of this mental view are nearly indistinguishable from memories of reality. These memories are not made quickly—they take time. But consistent revisiting of this mental view is retained in our memories just like the real thing.

Using visualization to create memories is effective when the visualization is believable. However, when the mental picture is at odds with our other experiences, then visualized memories fail. Visualizations, when unbelievable, encounter rejection from the reasoning parts of our brain. Our logic generates neural signals—this "doesn't fly"—and associated visual images are discarded as a long-term memory. In addition, distrust often activates our instinct to survive, and in the workplace, this always results in diminished results and frequently in attrition. It is likely you have experienced this yourself.

- Think about some experience in which you had a competent leader who painted a viable story then put in the work to make it real.
- Think about a different experience in which a less competent leader told you an implausible story—perhaps they left out key facts, perhaps they distorted the truth to tell you what they thought you wanted to hear.

Ask yourself about the first experience: Did the picture feel real? Did you feel trust, with time? Likely so. Ask yourself about the second experience: Did the picture feel real? Did you feel trust, with time? Likely not, and this is your brain's reasoning function doing its job.

Reality says, we rarely have all the answers all the time. Leaders are constantly tempted to "have all the answers." Don't be tempted to distort the truth. Don't just tell people what they want to hear. Don't omit key relevant facts or make implausible claims—these are counterproductive.

*So, what do we do with this information?*

- Deliberately paint a picture of a successful project with achievable success criteria.
- Be honest, be credible. If you don't know, just say, "I don't know."
- It's fine to attack big goals: "These are big goals, and we will get there by dis-assembling big intractable problems into smaller workable problems. We can expect some problems along the way, and we will work together to get past them. Our success criteria are well understood and achievable."
- Everyone needs a place and everyone needs a purpose, so paint the picture including the people and skills to accomplish the project success criteria.

Visualization and story, when credible, plant that visualized picture into our long-term memories, nearly indistinguishable from real long-term memories.

Visualization works when the story has credibility and when the storyteller is respected and trusted.

---

**KEY LEARNING**

» Don't lie.
» Don't treat people like they are disposable.

## 1.4 Multimodal Learning and Our Brains

- As a child, did you like to be read to? Why?
- TV is more engaging than radio. Why?
- Meetings in person are more engaging than phone calls. Why?
- Slides with diagrams are more engaging than slides with just text. Why?

Before spoken language, humans used a primitive set of gestures, facial expressions, and body language. We feel better connected after a face-to-face meeting, especially over food. This is deeply engrained into our communication and emotional wiring. Therefore, it is highly relevant to remote teams, as we communicate best in person, when we can hear vocal intonations, see facial expressions, and feel the body language. The simple answer is: these all involve multiple senses—sight, sound, and smell.

Seeing facial expressions along with hearing the voices is "multimodal sensory input." We learn in much the same way. Hearing the lecturer and seeing the diagrams and bulleted text is multimodal learning. It triggers different parts of our brain.

Multimodal learning is crucial in remote teams. A video call, with participants hearing the speech and seeing the facial expressions of others, improves engagement, improves retention, and improves our primitive sense of community. This multimodal experience resonates so much more than a phone call or an email, which involve only one sense.

The relevance for remote teams is: use video conferencing as much as possible and be persistent with your team to also turn on their cameras.

*Fast forward to modern remote teams:* We communicate best when several senses are engaged. We communicate best when we both see and hear each other.

I have found Microsoft® Teams® is very easy to use: click the teammate's name, call. It's easier than dialing a phone number, it's easier than writing an email. Your teammate gets to see you on video, sense your body language, your smile, the warm tone of your voice; hear your sense of humor. Connecting is healthy.

Don't assume calls are bothering anyone. Calls are valuable in ways emails are not.

Ever notice how easy it is for us to misinterpret the emotional tone of an email? Ever notice how we can apply a negative filter on email, even when neither the email nor the sender are negative? Emotional tones can be encouraging, helpful, considerate; *or* they can be critical, un-helpful, and inconsiderate.

Avoid email threads with lots of people. In the end, long email threads usually just die without any tangible outcome. The better alternative is to do a team video call with a supporting agenda, and follow up.

---

**BEST METHODS**

- » Video conferences, *camera on—every time!*
- » Video engages multiple senses. We pay attention. We understand more. We retain more. Use video *every time.*

## 1.5 Setting Up for Success, Becoming

Our instincts seek that visual picture of success. And that picture of success stimulates the parts of our brain that drive our ambition, our pride in a job well done, our professional egos.

The anticipation of success is exactly what Pavlov proved. The bell rang, the dog salivated in anticipation of success (getting fed).

In a foot race, can you find the will to run harder when you see the finish line? Exactly.

Let's invest a moment to explore the consequences of ignoring the picture of success—more specifically, the consequences of ignoring measurable project outcomes (we will cover outcomes and outputs later in the book).

If we ignore that picture of success and if we fail to share it, we deprive the team of a shared and common goal; this makes for poor/high-friction collaboration. This is nothing short of dereliction of duty, in that we set everyone up for failure. Everyone—your team, yourself, your company, your sponsor, and your customers—all set up for failure. It's the responsibility of the team lead to find that picture of success, those two or three things that define success—those two or three things that clearly show the finish line. Recognize that the impact of changing that success criteria is just like changing the finish line in a foot race. Avoid, at all costs, changing the criteria.

Successful projects *always* start with goals (aka, problem statements and measurable success criteria). Shared goals are the basis of healthy teams. Building anything of substance needs more than one individual. People solve problems. Process doesn't solve problems, nor do tools, nor do overbearing managers.

This seems so obvious when we say it out loud. But we still see short-sighted, self-centered managers pressure their teams in a misguided attempt to save money or do more with less. Isn't the project more important than potential savings? These managers naïvely prioritize saving money as more important than project success. It's most likely that the manager is thinking about the perception of overspending and ignoring the accountability for the project.

Let's focus on the positive—let's focus on project success. Successful projects all start with a clear vision of success. The mission of Apollo 11 was, "Send three men to the moon and back." I heard Neil Armstrong quip, "Let's not downplay that '*and back*' part." That project had a great vision, which lives on a half-century later.

Our project story is important; it deserves attention and refinement. Paint the picture of the project complete with the conclusion, ending with project results. Include the plan, clear to everyone, with reasonable time to complete the work. A team in which each person clearly knows what they are being tasked to accomplish. A team in which individuals can get help when needed. And a team with shared goals, all pulling on the same end of the rope. The story is one of team results, team accountability, not of individual performance.

Painting the picture of project results, shared team goals and measurables increases mental engagement. Our "community wiring" allows us to embrace teamwork and team accountability rather than individual performance. Painting the picture of the project clarifies that it is about team accomplishments and outcomes, not about the team leader, and definitely not about some uninvolved executive.

Clarity and stability are keystones. Keeping the project clear, stable, and unchanging accomplishes this. Guard against project instability and change, as these disallow the project story to be clear and compelling in the minds of your teammates. It is critical for effective remote teams to use the power of story to paint this clear, positive, and motivating picture in the minds of your teammates.

### 1.5.1 Achievable Goals and Success Criteria

Quality is seen through the eyes of the customer, user, consumer.

Diminishing returns means investing work into details that are not meaningful, and often not even visible, to the customer. Key results criteria should embrace this, with results measured in the achievable, not the perfect. Business dictates that your work product exceed the expectations of your customer, reader, or user, but that does not equate to zero bugs.

The very definition of diminishing returns is setting unreachable goals. Be sensitive to plans with goals requiring *perfection*.

- Few bugs are accomplishable, but zero bugs are likely diminishing returns.
- If current profit margins are 33%, then key success criteria 35% GM is accomplishable.
- But key success criteria of 50% GM is likely diminishing returns.
- As profit and revenues are somewhat inversely related, key success criteria of lower profit percentage with higher margins and higher gross profit is reasonable. But key success criteria of increased percentage profits, gross profits, and revenues is likely unrealistic.

About unreachable goals: If executives pass these types of goals down, it's worthwhile to ask, "Has this ever been accomplished by us in the past? Has this ever been accomplished in our industry in the past?" If the answer is, "Yes, it has," that leads to a healthy conversation about how they did it, the associated time, money, and business results. If the answer is, "No," that leads to a conversation about setting the company and the team up for success, not failure.

About diminishing returns: Teams and team members have been known to "polish the cannonball," meaning they invest time in valueless improvements. And value is seen through the eyes of the customer.

As you hear your team discuss their work, you may simply ask,

- "Will it significantly remedy customer pain or will it cause significant customer delight?"

When we discuss causes and remedies of customer pain, that's the opportunity to learn and improve.

Key learning: Set achievable goals. We are wired to survive, belong, and become. Success criteria, achievable and clearly stated, is an incredibly powerful tool to create that shared sense of purpose (appealing to our instinct to belong) and big ambitions and achievable goals (appealing to our instinct to become).

 A simple, powerful picture of results and team success triggers our dopamine response. This makes us feel more positive, increases focus, increases ability to learn, increases motivation and ambition.

**GOOD PRACTICES**

» Deal with unreachable goals by breaking the project into stepping stones, which eventually accomplish the goals.

» Don't move the finish line. A stable plan of record is imperative for a successful team and matters *more* for remote teams. Avoid constantly changing goals by keeping projects small and short. Change requests get pushed into the next release.

## 1.5.2 Criticism and Self-Criticism

From *How to Win Friends and Influence People*[6]:

"... [N]inety-nine times out of a hundred, people don't criticize themselves for anything, no matter how wrong it may be.
Criticism is futile because it puts a person on the defensive and usually makes him strive to justify himself.
Criticism is dangerous, because it wounds a person's precious pride, hurts his sense of importance, and arouses resentment."

The alternative is to offer guidance rather than criticism. There are often reasons things are not to your satisfaction. When that happens, first seek to understand—ask the "why" of the situation. Next offer your guidance, speak with respect, offer help, offer examples, suggest they do more of "X" and do less of "Y."

In situations in which it is difficult for you to find respect for your teammates, this is simply an indicator that you should put in the extra work and attention to

---

[6] Carnegie, A., 1936.

accomplish that mutual respect. The alternative is perceived or implied criticism, which leads to an absence of inspiration and motivation.

---

**BEST METHODS**

> » Guidance, do more of "X," do less of "Y" consistent with project goals; always bring it back to goals.
> » This is why it is so important to write, review, and avoid changing goals.
> » Make a conscious effort to genuinely respect your teammates, and they will usually find a way to respect you in return.

## 1.6 Mentoring, the Secret Weapon to Belonging

Mentoring is your *secret weapon* to build healthy, functional, efficient teams. We yearn for a place and a purpose, and mentoring touches both of these instincts.

Sharing the project story further cements it into our memories. And when we get help, that gives individuals confidence that they will play their role, successfully.

When we receive mentoring, we experience gratification that our mentor invests time, interest, and effort in us. This affirms that we are valuable to the team. Mentoring, knowledge, and practice increases our skill and confidence. In turn, this increases our eagerness to engage and contribute to the team.

When we mentor others, we experience gratification that our knowledge, skills, and wisdom have importance—that a student will both invest time and find value in this learning. This affirms our value to the team, and the student has affirmation that they too are of value.

### 1.6.1 How to Start

- Prime the pump by setting an example to those receiving mentoring. Just ask. You can ask for a mentor in something that you don't know well; if your strengths are in business, ask for mentoring in tech. Or if your strengths are in tech, ask for mentoring in business. When you say, "I could really benefit from deeper understanding of the coding challenges you encounter," you acknowledge you can learn and grow, you acknowledge there are others more skilled in this topic than you are. In essence, you are saying, "I don't know everything," and it is amazing how far this simple act of humility, of willingness to listen and learn, will go with your credibility in the group. This serves true whether you are team lead or in some other role. Be humble, listen, learn. It's a good example to set.

- Also prime the pump by setting an example for mentors. After you have asked for mentoring, immediately offer mentoring. Pick a topic or three and offer a session; it can be one on one, lunch and learn, or some other format.
- A real example: I have been fortunate to be in a position to write patents for my employers. Most early career people have mental blocks about patents. They don't know what is or is not patentable. They are unfamiliar with the subject matter expertise required; they often assume they must know everything about everything. I organized an optional lunchtime meeting. It was attended by two early career coworkers. I walked them through an example of the invention disclosure, the legal team involvement, and the final patent submission. We closed on a happy note, that patents are a "body of work" career item and worthwhile.
- Along the way, it's good to bring up mentoring during team meetings. This can be informal, perhaps during the "around the table" part of the agenda. Or it can be formal and a part of the agenda at which others report topics, progress, etc. The point: mentoring is important, and it should be frequently discussed and valued.

 When we receive mentoring, our instincts to belong are gratified. When we receive mentoring, our instincts to become are gratified.

**BEST METHODS**

» Talk about mentoring during team meetings. We all have a range of skills, talents, and experiences. Everyone has something to share, something to offer. Prime the pump by asking for mentoring and offering to mentor others.

## 1.7 The Power of Empathy and Our Wiring

Every significant accomplishment requires people.

Early on, it's easy to be excited about a shiny new project that will change the organization and change the world.

Later, holding the focus of teammates is much more challenging. Reality sinks in, team members encounter and struggle with the work, the obstacles, the dependence on others, and the imperfect communications and personalities of us all. The challenge is keeping every individual on the team consistently inspired and engaged *over the long haul.*

The magic of long-term engagement is simply desire. In teammates who desire success, the belong-and-become wiring will continue to produce. And teammates who don't have the desire will lose interest.

 Being remote magnifies our feeling of being alone. Empathy creates community and a feeling of belonging. These diminish our survival response.

**GOOD PRACTICES**

» The challenge for the team leader is to generate and maintain that desire to belong and become. For years, we have heard of managing by wandering around (MBWA), which can be a one-way conversation: "Tell me what you are working on," or it can be a genuine empathy builder: "Are you feeling good about things here at work? Do you have everything you need?"
» I care about you.
» I care enough to make myself available to hear your concerns and to have a social interaction.
» People are wired with a need to be heard and seen.
» Involvement and inspiration improve when concerns can be safely aired.

## 1.8 Trail Map and Conclusion

• Humans are illogical. We have primitive wiring and 4,000 generations of evolution. Our primitive wiring is not going to change, but we can change the way we interact with others, to know and manage our wiring to survive, to know and cultivate our need for a place and a purpose. Nurture wiring to belong and become.
• We all are wired to survive, and when our survival is threatened in any way, our survival wiring kicks in. The brain chemistry of our survival wiring precludes our abilities to use other parts of our brains to think rationally.
• We are wired to make snap judgments, to quickly judge "friend or foe"; when people don't look like us or don't sound like us, our snap judgments often say "foe."
• The remedy is to consciously counterbalance these negative responses. First, avoid triggering the survival response. Second, make a conscious effort to include, listen to, and respect those who don't look or sound like us.
• The positive wiring is where we make a significant contribution. We are all wired to need a place (a team with shared goals) and a purpose (tasks which are both challenging and realistic).

- Team leads are responsible for shaping the project and shaping the key success criteria. This key success criteria is the bell to Pavlov's dog. The key success criteria is the attainable finish line, the thing the team works for together.
- Mentoring each other is a secret weapon for building healthy teams.
- Empathy—consistent, *genuine* empathy for each other—is the other secret weapon for building healthy teams.
- The reward for all involved: consistent execution, absence of drama.

These benefit the organization and the contributors alike.

# Chapter 2

# Building Healthy Teams

In a perfect world, teamwork sets aside our individual agendas in the interest of our collective best interest. This conflicts with our deeply ingrained wiring to put our self-interest first.

Conscious effort is required by all—team leads, contributors, observers, and executive sponsors—to put self-interests aside and put team interests first. This bears repeating:

Conscious effort—team interests first, individual interests are subordinate.

These team interests and healthy teams will need efficient methods, processes, and tools to achieve the interests of the team and accomplish the significant. We are here to accomplish significant, right? So, we deal with the methods, processes, and tools to achieve the interests of the team. Otherwise, it's just "be nice" and don't worry about achieving anything.

Teams do not live by Zoom® alone. Putting people into a room or simply telling them to work together *never* results in a successful outcome. It takes work, and a reasonable time, to clarify the goals, to convert participants from observers to contributors to collaborators. This is harder when remote, but it is very possible with the right approach.

In this section we will cover tools, how to apply the tools, and the team skills necessary to achieve the desired outcomes.

## 2.1 Waterfall or Agile . . . Both or Neither?

Agile and waterfall are software methodologies. They are tools, not the main event. How leaders and teams apply these tools to accomplish the team goals, the shared outcomes, are the main events.

In the early days of software development, there was no process. Eight out of ten tech projects failed. It amounted to "ready, fire, aim," and repeat the same behavior, again and again, expecting different results.

## 2.1.1  Waterfall

Then the waterfall method was invented; it looks something like this:

```
Waterfall SW Development Process

→ Requirements
        → Design
                → Coding/implementation
                        → Testing/Verification
                                → Operations/Maintenance

   |                    ← Timeline To-Be-Determined →                    |
```

I've personally used waterfall on many projects. Waterfall is great, as we focus on *requirements* first and then design+implement. Waterfall avoids "ready, fire, aim." You have requirements, you know the problems you will solve.

However, waterfall is less than perfect. It can take too long: the task of collecting and then prioritizing requirements is nearly infinite. It's difficult for perfectionist personalities to stop collecting data and start making decisions and writing code. Also, it is difficult for non-perfectionist personalities to do a thorough job of capturing and documenting requirements.

But waterfall is a great process if you and your team can put some reasonable boundaries on requirements collection and definition. If you identify when returns become diminishing, it becomes possible to avoid analysis paralysis.

## 2.1.2  Agile

The other mainstream software method is agile, or the scrum method.[1] Agile looks something like this:

---

[1]  https://dzone.com/articles/why-i-hate-scrum

```
Agile SW Development Process (2-ish week loop)

→ sprint planning (user stories)
        → daily scrum
                → sprint review
                        → sprint retrospective


|               ← 2 weeks →              |
                Repeat Cycle
```

Agile's strengths are many. It is action oriented, it delivers something to see and improve right away. Shorter timelines lead to higher success rates and reduced project requirement changes. So, agile's popularity is understandable.

However, agile's weaknesses are also many. It relies on user stories from seemingly anyone, rather than well-organized requirements collection from the target audience, creating a high likelihood of solving problems for the wrong target audience.

Agile is not great for devops' work–life balance. Working in agile feels like one forced march after another, often involving extra hours, just so management can claim, "We are pushing the SW group," when in reality, devops is just one sprint after another, absent the "why." Big picture organizational benefits are invisible. The process diminishes morale and motivation.

Agile is not so agile. Agile doesn't do well with anything longer than 15 days, and some things simply take longer. Agile doesn't do well with big dev teams. And agile doesn't work well with cross-functional participation.

A combination of waterfall and agile achieves better benefits and more consistent long-term benefits. This combination fits cross-functional teams with higher order *outcomes* (satisfied customers, increased market share), rather than increased *outputs* (lines of code, bugs found/fixed).

The combination of waterfall and agile is (IMHO) the best approach for most mid-sized projects. Collect the requirements, define the problems you will solve, keep the list short, keep the timeline short. Push new work requests into the next release in the interest of keeping the present release unmolested and on track—keeping the "vision of success" is critical.

The debate about waterfall or agile methods is really a question of the right tool for the job.

For a garden you would use a garden trowel, not a backhoe in a flowerpot. For roadwork you would use a backhoe, not garden trowel. (See Figures 2.1a and 2.1b.)

**Figure 2.1**   Use a Trowel for Gardening, a Backhoe for Roadwork (*Source:* pixfuel.com)

---

**BEST PRACTICES**

» Use the methods that work for the team and the task.
» Appeal to our instinct to belong by encouraging people to ask for help. Celebrate mistakes, celebrate collaboration and breakthroughs that take the team closer to the key success criteria. Team results matter.
» Appeal to our instinct to become by painting that clear and unchanging picture of success. Shape the process so that it focuses on solving the problems at hand.

◊ Strong brain chemistry is at work.
◊ Strong developers concerned with survival and individual recognition complain about helping weaker developers. They assume their survival is reduced when they don't individually stand out.
◊ The value of strong developers is increased by "power metrics," business results, team results. The value of helping others is noticed and valued. Helping others itself is its own reward.

## 2.1.3 Agile and Effective Remote Teams

Folksy wisdom: When we buy a drill, it's not because we need a drill, rather it's because we need a hole.

This is a question of craftsmanship. Agile is a tool. The work product is about how we use the tool (it's a group effort). Applying agile tools and processes for remote teams is a skill, a craft to master. We are improving your craft and career skills to build effective, high-morale remote teams. And we are improving your organizational capabilities to deliver compelling products.

This is not a "nice to have." It's not an overstatement to call effective remote teams' capabilities and global talent pools "essential" to compete in the digital economy and Industry 4.0. (See Tables 2.1a and 2.1b.)

I did product management and program management before agile had been conceived or published. My on-the-job training involved user groups (customers) who gave me product feedback. I wrote these down for the developer teams, and they looked a lot like user stories.

I learned that long-duration projects failed more frequently than short projects. We broke big projects into smaller, shorter, consistently successful projects (aka, sprints).

And even before agile, we had remote people working in other offices: contractors, partners, and the like. These are not new problems, and craftsmanship to solve these problems is getting better all the time.

**Table 2.1a  Agile Manifesto Values, Relevance to Remote Teams**

| AGILE Manifesto 4 VALUES | Relevance to Effective Remote Teams |
|---|---|
| Individuals and interactions ARE VALUED over processes and tools | With remote teams, we need to make a conscious effort to interact with each other one on one. Without talking frequently, we fail each other and fail the team. Team results matter more than individual results. |
| | Do the processes and tools, but only as they benefit the team. |
| | Don't over-obsess or over-invest in tools for the sake of tools. |
| Working software IS VALUED over comprehensive documentation | Software will be used. |
| | Documentation is rarely read. |
| | Do the docs, but don't over-invest. |
| Customer collaboration IS VALUED over contract negotiation | Yes, collaborate with the customer. More collaboration is better. Focus on the problems, avoid dictated solutions. |
| | Do a plan of record. Push new requests into the next dev cycle (this mostly eliminates mission creep and avoids failed projects). |
| Responding to change IS VALUED over following a plan | Keep projects short. Avoid mission creep. |
| | Maintain a roadmap to capture future requests. |
| | Respond to change by prioritizing next project/ release rather than altering the current project WIP. |
| | In remote teams, communication is more important than ever. Stable projects reduce the risk of crossed wires and miscommunication—especially important to remote teams. |

### Table 2.1b  Agile 12 Principles, Relevance to Remote Teams

| AGILE 12 Principles | Relevance to Effective Remote Teams |
|---|---|
| Customer satisfaction by early and continuous delivery of valuable software | Project-related connections and interactions create that "picture of success" we are wired for; this is essential for remote teams. Frequent deliveries and continuous feedback are healthy.<br><br>Avoiding interaction and hiding behind a monitor is not healthy.<br><br>Suggestion: a customer feedback tool (such as a message box) that the whole team can view (and respond to the customer every time). Another opportunity to interact with the customer. |
| Welcome changing requirements, even in late development. | More customer interaction is healthy. Use short releases and roadmap. Show customers you listen and take action. Set reasonable expectations and clearly show customers that you deliver on commitments (customers will interact more, not less) |
| Deliver working software frequently (weeks rather than months) | Use short releases to avoid mid-project change of POR<br><br>New requests go into the roadmap for next projects rather than disrupting current project.<br><br>For any team, constant project changes lead to project failure. For remote teams, imperfect communications related to constant project changes significantly increase the risk of project failure. |
| Close, daily cooperation between business people and developers | Being remote means reduced feedback. Morale and productivity improve when remote teams know their work is relevant and valued. This is all in addition to the business value of delivering the proper solution. We are wired to have pride in our work. |
| Projects are built around motivated individuals, who should be trusted | Truer words have never been spoken. When we encounter lack of clear goals (or constantly changing goals), micromanagement, and low morale, these point to a failure in management. When we scratch the surface, we usually find<br><br>• Cost control, internal rather than external/customer focus<br><br>• Micromanagement, weak functional management, top down management<br><br>• High talent attrition, not great people/skills remaining<br><br>For remote teams, micromanagement, top-down project changes lead to imperfect communications, significantly increasing the risk of project failure. |
| Face-to-face conversation is the best form of communication (co-location) | For remote teams, use video conferencing, every time, including one-on-ones.<br><br>Morale matters—we are building a sense of place and purpose. |

*Continues on next page*

**Table 2.1b  Agile 12 Principles, Relevance to Remote Teams *(cont.)***

| | |
|---|---|
| Working software is the primary measure of progress | For remote teams, tools matter: regular builds, structured testing, consistent defect logging/resolution. |
| Sustainable development, able to maintain a constant pace | For any team, and especially remote teams, avoid the cycle of overload, then idleness. Agile avoids situations in which work piles up and then lands hard on one or two team members without adequate time to complete. Use agile task boards with short tasks, quick and consistent hand offs, and end customer input (see the penny game in the Appendix). |
| Continuous attention to technical excellence and good design | Agile fast handoffs create more learning. For remote teams, handing code from member to member increases interaction and learning, even when people don't share the same office. |
| Simplicity—the art of maximizing the amount of work not done—is essential | Remote teams always face communication problems. Keeping tasks simple, keeping projects short, and avoiding changes makes remote team execution significantly more efficient. |
| Best architectures, requirements, and designs emerge from self-organizing teams | This is essential. Knowledge work is complex. The people closest to the problem—immersed in the problem—will provide the optimal architectures, requirements, designs, and end user interactions.<br><br>Top-down management simply lacks the knowledge. |
| Regularly, the team reflects on how to become more effective and adjusts accordingly | Healthy teams celebrate mistakes, learn, and improve. BUT this requires a "team first" meritocracy. It doesn't work well with an "individual first" meritocracy, or no meritocracy at all. |

*Source:* https://en.wikipedia.org/wiki/Agile_software_development

## 2.2  Plan of Record (POR) and Remote Teams  •

A Plan of Record (POR) is essential whether you use agile, or waterfall, or something else. The surest way to have a project fail is to keep changing the plan. So, if you'd like your project to succeed (and who doesn't), then don't change the plan.

- Clarify the plan, yes.
- Course correct the plan, yes.
- Risk management, yes.
- Vague plan, stale POR, or no plan of record—*no!*

### 2.2.1  Unpacking a POR: Start with the End in Mind

Simply ask yourself, "What does success look like?"

This is admittedly a tech project POR, but a project is anything with a start, a finish, and some desired outcome. Accordingly, this POR approach is workable for tech products such as hardware or commercial software and is applicable for in-house IT projects, business projects, education projects, research projects (anything with a start/finish/outcome).

- **Scope.** The big picture project.
- **Key success criteria (power metrics):** Improve customer survey feedback by (X), expand customer usage by (Y), improve gross profit by ($Z).
- **Constraints:** Known constraints beyond a feature list. These include cost of materials constraints, costs of R&D constraints, quality metrics, compatibility, schedule. Go to market, or deployment, knowledge exchange and training, pricing, sales playbooks, partner training, marketing promotion, awareness and demand.
- **Outside of scope:** As the name says, work which is specifically NOT in the project, or work to be done by others. I have been on tech projects that explicitly said "no new silicon."
- **Project work breakdown:** Breaking those big tasks into smaller, manageable tasks with resources, schedule, and known dependencies.
- **POR project staging:** Everything need not be done at once. A good POR will define the release 1.0 and also have a working definition for release 2.0 and 3.0. Call it staging, call it a roadmap, whatever suits the situation. Smaller project stages greatly increase the chance of successful execution, and smaller project stages work to avoid project changes. You will get requests to expand the project scope, and it's best to say, "Version 1 is close to release. We will find a home for your request in version 2." The best way you can ensure project success is to avoid mission creep. Put those requests in the next version, every time.

From personal experience, well-conceived tech projects can fail after acknowledged R&D success in which the features, quality, and schedule were all met. The projects failed for lack of post-R&D execution such as marketing, sales enabling, awareness and demand. This matters more for remote teams, because a clear POR (including business results) puts everyone into a stable, well-understood situation: "I know what my bits are, I know what your bits are too." Without this stability, primitive and survival emotions take over and displace frontal lobe logical thinking. With a clear plan of record with business results, the team is typically more willing to engage with sales. Marketing, ops, deployment—they only need clarity on what's expected. In addition, assume your teammates have other demands on their time. We cover that shortly.

We have heard, "People don't quit companies, people quit managers," so put yourself in the shoes of the remote teammate. Without a stable POR, you are constantly unclear about what's to be done. You don't feel connected to "the community" and are potentially over-sensitive to criticism, leading to a downward spiral, which results in poor performance or attrition.

## 2.2.2 Define Problems, Don't Dictate Solutions

### From Personal Experience

Early in my career, I was a product manager for geographic information software (GIS) (think city utility layout). I was asked to run a steering committee meeting. It was 15 city government utilities services senior managers and myself.

I had my pen and yellow notepad, and said, "OK, what would you like to talk about?" And I was bombarded with minutiæ: We want a report about "abc," we want a button to do "def," we want a user interface for "ghi" . . . minutiæ . . . hours of it.

I took furious notes, captured every detail I could. I also said, "I hear you on the need for 'abc'; please help me better understand the problem you are solving." Magic.

I went back to the software team with a document with mandatory problem statements, supported by suggested/optional implementation (the button, or report, or UI).

We did a page turner, and the software team responded favorably. They had enough whitespace to work some magic. And with spiffy software architecture skills, they *exceeded* the requirements—all of them. The developers were super happy. The customers were super happy. And it was due to a single, simple approach:

*Tech folks want to solve problems.* So, give them a reasonably well-defined problem to solve and success criteria and get out of their way. Let them work their magic. Do a team review with the non-tech folks to give the developer a valued place at the team table, and give the non-tech folks greater understanding and context so that they may excel in their jobs as well. This is especially important in remote teams.

## 2.2.3 Dealing with Uncertainty: What We Might Do, What We Will Do

Every project starts with a debate on "what we *might* do," and that's healthy and serves a good purpose. But your team will need to determine "what we *will* do." Fortunately, it comes back to goal setting and key success criteria. When you bring up goals and success criteria, you can expect your team to want to skip past it. You will hear something like, "We already understand the problem, no need to elaborate on the obvious." The team leader set-aside is, "You probably know this already . . . just want to review so everyone has shared understanding and everyone understands the big picture." The subtext: review leads to discussion and questions. A goals review and workshop discussion increases engagement and clarifies the mental picture of success.

A healthy "what we might do" and "what we will do" debate creates an opportunity for teammates to contribute; it will paint that picture of how we manage risk together, what tools and resources we will need, what we will learn as individuals, and what we will learn as a team. The journey and what we will learn as a team will trigger our instinct-to-become brain wiring. There are few psychological rewards as powerful as a shared and successful journey as a group.

At this critical point, team leaders have a choice. They can define problems, or they can dictate solutions.

*Occam's razor:* A philosophy of problem solving: "Make things as simple as possible, but no simpler."[2]

Occam's razor advocates *abductive heuristic,* a fancy term for "observe and then do a practical solution." If that attempt at a practical solution or prototype fails, you learned something—move on and attempt something else. If it succeeds, less than perfect/suboptimized is acceptable.

When dealing with uncertainty, perfection and complexity are not your friends. When dealing with uncertainty, the POR is your friend, simplicity is your friend, and your roadmap is your friend. As elegant/complex solutions arise that create schedule or resource problems, these solutions have value and can be captured in the roadmap's next revision. Roadmaps take time and effort, communication and buy-in. The reason roadmap efforts are worthwhile is project stability and future prioritization.

The roadmap should be as simple and low friction as possible but still get the central task done (see Table 2.2).

We envision a simple document format, no need to indulge in graphics, unless it really floats your boat. This is an opportunity to focus on "*why,*" rather than on "*what.*" Roadmaps should focus on problem statements and outcomes. Roadmaps should avoid dictating solutions: give developers and other contributors some whitespace, give them some ability to think for themselves and solve the problem their own way—you will be pleasantly surprised.

The roadmap also serves to prioritize and focus, while still allowing team discussions about alternative topics (out of scope). At the end of team discussions, it is simple to confirm:

Great discussion, we agreed there are no changes to the plan for release 1,
OR great discussion, we agreed to change the plan for release 1.

---

2  Wikipedia: https://en.wikipedia.org/wiki/Occam's_razor

## Table 2.2 Example Roadmap

| Example Roadmap (Relentless Prioritization, Stability and Execution) | | |
|---|---|---|
| Release 1 | Objectives and outcomes | thing 1.1 – problem statement, constraints<br>thing 1.2 – problem statement, constraints<br>thing 1.3 – problem statement, constraints |
| Release 2 | Objectives and outcomes | thing 2.1 – problem statement, constraints<br>thing 2.2 – problem statement, constraints<br>thing 2.3 – problem statement, constraints |
| Release (future) for prioritization | Objectives and outcomes | thing F.1 – problem statement, constraints<br>thing F.2 – problem statement, constraints<br>thing F.3 – problem statement, constraints |

And so, the team gets to have those creative discussions, without creating confusion on what will or will not be prioritized.

With a roadmap as a landing zone for future requests, the immediate project stays stable. When the project is initially conceived, it takes time and effort to define the scope, align with business goals, and establish key success criteria. In addition, it took time and effort to engage the team, build their understanding, and build their shared view of success. It's not advisable to keep changing the project, moving the goalposts, and messing with the team's stability and confidence. Good roadmap management is the remedy.

If you see a project or team without a clearly stated mission and clearly stated outcomes, that's a red flag. Assuming the positive, get the team involved in clarifying and writing these out—it will be good for them. But if they don't manage to get it done themselves, something else is wrong, and you should provide some help to attain that necessary clarity. More on roadmaps later in the book.

 A consistent and unchanging mental picture of success appeals to our instincts to belong to a successful team, and our instincts to become by contributing to the project and the team. BUT constantly changing the plan only results in engaging our survival instinct, which shouts down our more positive instincts.

**BEST PRACTICES**

» Don't mess with this immediate project; rather, capture those feature requests into a future release. Constantly changing the plan, changing the success criteria, creates high risk of project failure.

### 2.2.4 The Well-Executed Risk Management Plan

This matters more for remote teams because being separated from our community increases the sensitivity of our survival response.

Normally, when a team leader says "risk management," we think of technical challenges, quality assurance, end-user adoption, and the like. However, risk for remote teams takes on a new meaning. Contributor morale is now a bigger risk. Fortunately, this is understandable and manageable. Remote teammates experience a feeling of disconnect/isolation. This is an additional component of risk management, but it is manageable with a bit of attention.

### 2.2.5 The Merit of Short Projects, Not One Large Heavy Project

Short projects are, well, short, and easier to show results. Showing results early and often gives the team confidence, provides team visibility to executive leadership. In turn, executive leadership confidence improves.

Short projects have the hidden benefit of avoiding constant project change. It is normal for a team to encounter project change requests. In fact, an absence of change requests is a negative indicator on stakeholder understanding or business value.

So, be welcoming of change requests, and do your best to deliver sooner rather than later. With short projects, you have the luxury of pushing change requests into the next release—and the next release will happen soon. The conversation is much simpler: "Project 1.0 is on track for release in a short time. Your request will be added to Project 2.0. OK?"

Short timelines are our friends. This results in a simpler task of ongoing *value prioritization*. Value prioritization is a simple concept: look at the value of the requested improvement, look at the associated expense. Sort the list based on high value and low cost. Draw the line, and that's the scope of version 2.0. Prioritize those tasks based on benefit and expense. That's a roadmap.

In contrast, big projects with long schedules are significantly more likely to have forced changes to the project plan, simply because some new requests cannot wait. Project changes cause setbacks, re-architecting, re-planning, and project churn.

For effective remote teams, shorter projects with quick results improve engagement and better visibility between the teams, leadership, and stakeholders.

---

**GOOD PRACTICES**

» A stable POR matters more for remote teams. Bite-sized projects are your friends.

» Avoid constantly changing goals by keeping projects small and short. Change requests get pushed into the next release.

A simple, powerful picture of results and team success triggers our dopamine response. This makes us feel more positive, increases focus, increases ability to learn, increases motivation and ambition.

## 2.3 On-Boarding and Team Formation

The old joke, "When making breakfast, the hen is involved, but the pig is committed," is a high-contrast comment on *involved* observers vs. *committed* contributors.

It's certainly fine to have observers, but let's not make the mistake of confusing observers for contributors.

### 2.3.1 Individual Accountability vs. Team Accountability

Our objective is team accountability, meaning the team shares the same goals, the same priorities. Team members do the work and materially contribute to the same goals and are not to be confused with observers.

On-boarding is especially relevant in remote teams. As a new contributor to the team, it takes significant will and energy to "cold call" a teammate and say, "Hi, I'm new, what should I do?" For remote teams, it is up to the team lead to relieve that burden; it will not magically happen without intention and a bit of effort.

For team leads, it is *so* worthwhile to invest time and effort into on-boarding.

- It is good for the team lead. Proper on-boarding requires a well-constructed project plan of record, key success criteria, people patterns, methods and communications. It tasks team leads in a healthy way.
- It is good for contributors. They know exactly what they will contribute. They know the plan, know the people, know the methods and communications. The result is that contributors will feel a part of the project, a part of the group.
- It is good for the team. The team knows what to expect of the contributor, the contributor is encouraged to improve (but avoid re-inventing) the project. The contributor builds trust in the team, and the team builds trust in the contributor.
- For everyone, proper on-boarding leads to healthier teams that are better equipped to manage through difficulty.

On-boarding is especially relevant in remote teams, because when we are alone, we frequently magnify negative stimuli and dismiss positive stimuli. For remote teams, it is up to the team lead to relieve the burden on the contributor. It will not magically happen without intention and a bit of effort.

### 2.3.2 Team Makeup and Functional Managers

Functional managers get involved as observers, which is OK as long as their observation leads to buy-in and assignment of material contributors. Functional managers are often risk averse, and given a choice, they will avoid risking limited resources just because you asked.

Even after contributors are assigned, it's critical for managers to understand the value of the project and the value of their team contribution. The risk if functional managers don't understand or value the project are that those resources will be eroded and redirected to other tasks. As you on-board contributors, here are questions to ask yourself and ask them.

- Contributor, are you on the team? Is this a priority for you?
- Contributor, can you participate in meetings, and do follow up?
- Contributor, is your manager on board?
- Contributor, will your manager pull you off to do something else?

The risk here is the manager, not the contributor.

Managers who have full-time staff answering to them have been known to invisibly redirect contributors they manage without the knowledge of the team lead.

Spotty resources are high on the list of reasons projects fail. Your project is a priority (period). If it's not a priority, just cancel the project and do something that *is* a priority. It is regrettable that this is the reason projects need executive sponsors. The functional manager will be motivated to avoid causing problems by redirecting committed staff to some other task. They are motivated to avoid criticism in the eyes of executives. In an ideal world, we would not need this ineffective appendix, but our world is less than perfect, and other perceived emergencies compete for priority. This applies to full-time staff; the equation changes when external contractors are involved. We cover how to make effective use of external contractors and other remote team contributors throughout this book.

Back to on-boarding. It's fine for managers to attend. Be clear about their role, however: are they observers or are they contributors? Encourage them to contribute something significant (code or content); they may surprise you—assume the positive.

### 2.3.3 Personal Experiences of Team On-Boarding

I was once "volun-told" to fix a dysfunctional team. This was not a remote team, but we will show how this applies to remote at the end of this section.

The participants were decent folks, all senior architects. As expected, they were all long on ego, but short on actual coding. They'd been chewing the fat for a year, with zero results to show.

I let the team know I had been tasked to do program management. Fortunately, my brain–mouth filter was functioning, and, tempting as it was, I did *not* say, "I was told to clean up this mess." Nor did I say I'd recover this profoundly broken goat-rope.

Rather, I attended a couple of team meetings just to get a feel for it. Since there was so much old baggage involved, I opted to start with the one-to-one approach.

There were 10 team members, and I organized an informal one-to-one with each of them. I asked them each the same four questions:

- What should I know about you? Tell me about yourself.
- How can you make the biggest contribution to the project?
- What is going well about the project?
- What might be improved about the project?

Let's review the logic behind the questions.

- **What should I know about you?** Tell me about yourself. Asking team members to tell me about themselves and their professional background shows I want to understand their strengths. I want to understand their mastery. Listen first, then understand, then talk.
- **How can you make the biggest contribution to the project?** Asking team members about how they can contribute shows I want to play people to their strengths, I hope to understand their views on what they can contribute, and I want to make assignments consistent with career directions.
- **What is going well about the project?** I respect and make good use of the work already performed and (assuming the positive) that there is good work to be found and that good work should be put to good use.
- **What might be improved about the project?** I am seeking their input on how we can improve, how everything can be improved. Notice I use no negative language. Nor do I suggest any reason to "throw away" the work. Trashing or devaluing previous work brings out the reactive, defensive lizard brains.

So, we look to fix that which can be fixed. Notice this is an engineering problem—their purpose and their place is restored.

For this project, nine out of ten folks told me later that the team benefited from that approach.

Humility with perseverance matters; a team lead doesn't have all the answers and is far from perfect. But we found a way to work together to find out what we didn't know and found better ways to cure customer pain.

## 2.3.4 Team Emergence, Getting Past the Adjustment Period

Teams all go through some getting started period, then an adjustment/conflict period, then a working together nicely period, and then a working together really well period (aka, the Tuckman Model: team forming, storming, norming, performing[3]). Tuckman helps us understand what to expect, but falls short:

- Why we form–storm–norm–perform
- How to help remote teams arrive at a state of "performing"
- How to help remote teams maintain and improve with time
- How to establish teams based on meritocracy and without bias
- How to establish an organizational culture based on global talent

Why teams go through *forming*: Surviving is easier when we have an accepting community. When we meet a new team, we feel positive as our need for a place and a purpose is fulfilled. But the need to survive eclipses our need for place and purpose. Our primitive wiring dictates that any negative stimuli such as harsh criticism = immediate negative stimuli, fear, flight. And positive stimuli such as a reward or group moment = positive but lower-priority stimuli, to be enjoyed later when threats are absent. Seemingly small negative stimuli shouts down any and all positive stimuli.

Why teams go through *storming*: When we start working with a new team, our competitive nature kicks in, and we strive to establish a place of higher importance in the pack. This creates conflict and drama—storming. When newly added members attempt to re-invent the project, this is an attempt to establish a spot of higher importance. Re-invention diminishes the prior work. If the person inflicting the re-invention wins, it is at the expense of the work of others. If the re-invention is allowed, the early team's value is diminished, business goals and timeline are jeopardized, and understandably lasting deep-seated negative feelings related to survival, belonging, and achievement will linger. We will get to the remedy shortly.

How teams get to *norming* and *performing*: When the team resolves the conflict and the drama evaporates, the team begins to work together with less friction, but falls short of working together effectively. Within reason, professional

---

3   https://en.wikipedia.org/wiki/Tuckman%27s_stages_of_group_development

conflict is a reality; there are always different ways to solve problems. Our task becomes how to deal with conflict in a healthy way. As conflict arises, the safe method is revisiting the goals and the definition of success. This "common ground" creates some shared agreement and shared goals.

At its essence, workplace conflict arises from our instincts to contribute and belong. It can (and often does) stimulate our instinct to survive, because if we anticipate that our idea will be rejected, at a very primitive level we feel rejected. Our instincts drive us to contribute to our community, and as we contribute, then we belong. And when our contributions are stepped on, our contribution is rejected, and we don't feel valued or have a sense of belonging.

Once we rehear the goal, it gives everyone whitespace to work with and room to contribute. We can better define the problem, and then conflicts about the best solution typically transition into discussions on collaboration to deliver on the goal.

All we did was "up level" the conversation to a restatement of the problem, which creates something both parties can agree on. And with agreement, the instinct to survive diminishes and now we appeal to the instinct to belong.

**GOOD PRACTICES**

- » Conflict will happen, that's a fact. Now what to do about it?
- » Create something all parties can agree on, some shared reality, some common vision.
- » Revisit the project goals and picture of success.
- » And remind all involved, problems can have many solutions. Once we agree on the goal and appeal to our instinct to belong, the survival instinct gets quiet, as the solution becomes a collaboration, rather than a conflict.

## 2.3.5 New Team Member On-Boarding Package

Frequently, team members join well after the team or project is underway. In the worst case, a new team member will "grab for the wheel"—attempt to re-invent the project and subordinate the other team members (by all means, lets avoid that dumpster fire).

Recognize that when new team members are added, they lack that clarity of goal, success criteria, and common vision shared by those who contributed to the project earlier. Accordingly, new team members can introduce new team conflict. The way to avoid, or at least diminish, conflict is to bring new team members up to speed quickly and efficiently.

Adding new teammates mid-project takes preparation and attention. Be well prepared to on-board new individuals in mid-project. Write an on-boarding package, *keeping goals and success criteria front and center.* Team resources, roles, and responsibilities are next. Then team processes: POR, specs, roadmap, voice of customer, status reports, DevOps, self-test. It's OK to have the new team member offer suggestions, with two caveats: the suggestions need to be consistent with success criteria, and the suggestions need to recognize other work that's been contributed.

Improvements on pre-existing: yes. Reinvention of pre-existing: no.

Frequent one-on-one meetings start with a page turner review of the goals and success criteria. The aim is to review risk management, initiate short projects, and develop the roadmap to avoid changing the POR. Encourage attendees to contribute.

While the forming–storming–norming–performing team evolution is 100% a valid model, it misses the point that teams usually start really small, and then, mid-project, teammates are added. This begs the question of how to best onboard these new teammates mid-project. The on-boarding package is really a project package, as this same body of information can also be used when teammates get lost in the weeds or, in other cases, for project observers.

---

**GOOD PRACTICES**

» Adding new teammates mid-project takes preparation and attention.
» Use on-boarding package with new teammate(s).
» Use one-on-one meetings and page turners of goals, success criteria, and other resources (aka, tools they can use to contribute). Allow them to ask questions. You can ask them questions on how they can best contribute.

---

 Paint the picture of goals and success. Show them how to contribute and belong and thereby, our instinct to belong is stimulated, collaboration is created. Our instinct to survive is quieted, conflict is avoided.

---

## 2.3.6 Lessons for Remote Team On-boarding

Remote teams are particularly sensitive to both positive and negative stimuli. Setting people up for success and playing to their strengths builds positive communal stimuli. Remote teams are particularly sensitive to survival stimuli; hence, it is best to avoid negative wording implying the project has failed. Objectivity when finding what's worth saving and worth fixing avoids survival stimuli.

Make a serious effort to play people to their strengths—simply asking what those strengths are is common sense. Regrettably, this is frequently overlooked in newly formed teams.

By avoiding negative language, we avoid stimulating survival wiring and the defensive response of the lizard brain.

---

**GOOD PRACTICES**

Try these lightly modified questions with your teams, one on one:
» Can you help me understand more about yourself? Can I better understand your mastery and your career path?
» Can you tell me if you might make a bigger contribution to the project?
» Can you help me better understand what's going right about the project and what might be improved?
This works very well with remote teams using one-to-one video calls. Use video to improve engagement, eye contact, and memorability for you both.

If you must assign non-core strength tasks, be deliberate and confirm to the contributor that you understand this is not their norm and you are not setting them up for criticism or failure.

Tasking people to do what they are eager to do is more common sense. It sets the project up for success, and on-boarding creates an appropriate opportunity to have these critical conversations. This is good for the project and the business, too.

## 2.3.7 On-boarding Global Talent and Bias

Our brains are wired to quickly put things into categories: "like us" or "not like us" is a deeply held instinct. For effective remote tech teams, we focus on meritocracy and results. This requires all of us to focus on the reality of meritocracy and results—nothing more and nothing less. We have all witnessed workplaces in which work was assigned based on favoritism, raises were given based on favoritism, promotions and firings were done based on favoritism. This is truly unfortunate to everyone involved, including those benefiting from the favoritism.

With favoritism:

• The non-favorites suffer through less desirable assignments, lower job satisfaction, being passed over for promotion and raises, or being fired.
• The teams suffer through witnessing the lack of meritocracy.
• The favorites and the people indulging in favoritism suffer long-term with the stress of assignments for which they lack the skills. They are less focused on results and more focused in avoiding blame—the very definition of a

dysfunctional and toxic workplace. For a sports metaphor, they are like a bad wrestler who is hard to pin but never wins.

- The company suffers from project delays, poor quality, project failures, lost revenues, and talent moving to employment by the competition. These companies, too, are like bad wrestlers who are hard to pin, but never win.

Meritocracy and results without bias and without favoritism:

- Those demonstrating merit collect the preferred assignments, have higher job satisfaction, receive justified promotions and raises.
- The teams win as they perform, and team members are motivated to perform with strong examples.
- Those with lower meritocracy are motivated to improve. Their managers are motivated to help them improve, to offer assistance and training to help them achieve higher merit.
- The company benefits from schedule integrity, higher quality, improved revenues, and attracting top talent.
- About bias in ourselves, we are naturally wired to categorize. When we make conscious efforts to disallow subconsciously categorizing those who don't look like us or speak like us as somehow inferior, we all win. Meritocracy is very possible when we focus on results, as measured through clear goals, as managed by competent and empathetic team leadership. With meritocracy, everyone wins.
- Dealing with bias in others is not easy but is worthwhile. With conscious effort we can create the right habits. We present facts based on project goals and metrics and suggest decisions based on meritocracy rather than favoritism. If we are even partially successful, we create an organizational capability and competitive advantage employing global talent.

With remote teams, it is far too easy to play favorites with teammates who are somehow "apart": whether racially diverse, with different language skills, or other "other" qualities. It is simply too easy to assign those folks the less desirable tasks and then pass them by for raises and promotions. If they are contract workers, it is easy to pass them by for longer-term work or pay increases. This hurts everyone and results in your organization's becoming less competitive at a time when competitors are likely successfully employing global talent pools.

## 2.3.8 Software Patterns—People Patterns

John Almon, CEO of The AI Platform, told me[4]:

---

[4] Personal email.

*Designing a team is like design patterns for object-oriented programming. You must optimize the skills sets as if they were function calls of the objects, and communication transfers between the individuals as if they are APIs . . .*

There is real merit in applying the wisdom of software engineering to project leadership. Software patterns use modules (aka, microservices). Each module has clearly defined inputs and outputs and independent unit testing. Projects and people can (and should) be organized in a similar fashion.

The hard science of Almon's approach makes sense. "People patterns" offer real clarity to every team member; they break a big problem into manageable components and apply folks with the right skills to the various components. These components are independent and measurable—they lend themselves to automated unit testing.

Regarding timeline and execution, Almon's approach allows each team member to get going with little or no waiting on others. The sooner any team member gets finished with a task, the sooner that team member can put in high-value contributions in other areas, including early starts on future improvements identified by the roadmap. That in itself is its own reward.

This approach offers real clarity on necessary communications between individuals, because it identifies module-to-module inputs and outputs. In the likely event that some change is mandated, the changes are isolated and have limited impact on other parts of the project. Project leadership hard science is well covered by this patterns approach.

## What About Non-Technical Participants?

Every financially successful project has other non-software functions such as tech training, tech pubs, competitive marketing, market launch, pricelist, manufacturing, sales training, sales reference account generation, and operations forecasting. Leadership can, and should, identify those non-software patterns, identify the inputs and outputs, and identify the people-to-people communications.

Start with "Why." People can be unwilling to get out of their comfort zones. You can expect to hear push back (or even passive resistance) along the lines of, "I'm software, why am I talking to sales?" or "I'm sales, why am I talking to software?" The response to the software folks can be:

*Why? The financial success of the project requires that we clearly communicate the value of this project. We build a brief training for the sales team, covering topics A, B, and C, emphasizing why this is "better and different."*

*This is an awesome project and our customers and partners need to know.*

*You(dev), Joe(sales), and I can meet to determine the outline. If you have any difficulty, ask for help.*

*Think of it as broadening your experiences and making new friends—they don't bite.*

*If it wasn't important, I wouldn't ask.*

This conversation answers "Why." It appeals to the person's sense of place and purpose. The meeting with the team lead's participation will bridge the gap between tech folks and sales folks. The meeting will generate a list of specific inputs and outputs. "Ask for help" means no one is being set up for failure. The closing sentences show the reward and the confidence.

The soft science of this equation also makes sense.

While we know that humans are illogical, emotional, unpredictable, and vain, we also know that humans respond to environments that appeal to our instincts to have a place and have a purpose.

The people patterns approach provides a clear part to play for each team member (including external resources). It provides real clarity into the big picture, which appeals to our instincts to be a part of something bigger than ourselves; it is inspiring and motivating.

The people patterns approach requires forethought and clarity from leadership. Both people pattern and software pattern approaches require writing down the architecture and the interfaces and establishing clear people patterns to match the software architecture, all focused on success criteria. This hard work is worth it; the alternative of no patterns and no clear responsibilities results in "toddler soccer," not teamwork, and certainly not effective execution.

**BEST METHODS**

>> Put the work into diagramming the project, tasks–inputs–outputs, including the non-code cross-functional bits.
>> Review people patterns with the team, just like a design review or code review. Make sure team input is heard (including remote and external folks).
>> Arrive at a plan of record for people pattern inputs/outputs.

## 2.3.9 On-Boarding Mid-Project and the Plan of Record

On-boarding happens a few people at a time, and of course, we encourage new people to ask questions, learn, and become engaged. This then triggers the dopamine (good) response, which improves mood, alertness, and the ability to learn.

On occasion, you may encounter the over-reach, whereby new people seek to redirect the project, usually without attempting to understand what's already there.

While it is critical that new people know their place and purpose on the team, it is equally critical that they respect the places and purposes of the people already on the team. It is critical that they respect the work that happened prior to their involvement. While we want and need the contributions of everyone, allowing the project to be re-invented every time someone new joins sets the remote team up for failure.

Fortunately, there is a good remedy. And the remedy is a *well-written plan of record (POR)*. A consistent POR lends connection and stability even when the team community is virtual and not face to face. Our objective is to give our team the same feeling of connectedness and stability they feel when sharing office settings. Office settings can be a crutch for weak project management; hallway conversations let us know if or when the project changes. Obviously, this hallway communication is harder with remote teams. This feeling of being out of the loop happens with remote contributors.

The team lead can improve connectedness by over-communicating the written POR. The magic of a written POR appears if/when plan changes. The team leader updates the written POR, makes that known to the team, discusses adjustments at team call, later discusses it again at team call to confirm it's understood and acceptable, and doesn't cause any other project changes, such as changed schedule, different skills, or risk.

A written POR also allows discussion and debate of alternatives without confusion. The team or team members can propose or comfortably debate alternative approaches. And at the end of the discussion, we clarify if we did, or did not, change the POR. This yields clarity of plan and allows debate while minimizing confusion. The same serves true for on-boarding new team members. A POR offers clarity on the decisions already made prior to their on-boarding. A POR allows them to debate previous decisions. Conversely, a POR disallows a re-invention of the project or undoing of previous work done. A POR also clarifies roles and responsibilities in the interest of respect for places and purposes of the folks already on the team.

---

**GOOD PRACTICES**

Help new teammates find their healthy place in the team without "blank page restarts."

» Respect team progress to date, respect those who did the work.
» Review what's there, improve on what's there, and no blank page restarts.
» Suggest a specific high-value task that will use pre-existing work.
» Give them license to improve/clarify/augment, and set a time for the new member to present new work to the team.
» Have a dry run if there are safety issues.

This will take several iterations until the conflict is gone.

### 2.3.10 Establishing the Team and Aligning Common Purpose

Expect negative filtering; you can expect to encounter those who filter any and all feedback as a personal attack, because they don't "feel safe" providing input. It is hard for them to be a part of the team community, and allowing this to continue results in dysfunction. Also, you can expect to encounter those who have no problem getting out of their lane, leaning into others without consideration, contradicting for no apparent reason.

There can be a mis-match on what they want to provide and what the team needs from them. We've all seen situations in which there has been reasonable progress or completion of a particular area of the project, and yet a team member "self-assigns" a redo from a blank page. This is likely that they are simply looking for a place in the community where they feel safe and valued.

Often a new individual is simply unaware there is pre-existing content, or has yet to read pre-existing content. A blank page restart amounts to a project setback. Take a deep breath; everyone (including us) has their own set of rough edges, some more pronounced than others.

Successful individual on-boarding means joining the team, in context. We have a game plan: study it first, contribute next.

- **Task 1.** Read the existing goals, objectives, and existing materials. Use team tools, POR, file sharing—point new teammate to existing work.
- **Task 2.** To foster understanding of the logic behind the plan, have the original author do a page turner.
- **Task 3.** Ask the new teammate to build on what's already there, to contribute improvements. Everything can benefit from improvement, everything can be added to, augmented, fleshed out, clarified.

The teammate has a need to belong to the team community. They need to feel safe when contributing suggestions and content. If they do not feel safe, then preparation, offline page turners, and dry runs will help. Yes, it takes time, but a healthy functional team is preferable to the alternative.

The result is that you are giving the new teammate a place and a purpose *and* you are preserving the place and purpose of others who did the original work.

<hr />

**GOOD PRACTICES**

» A stable POR allows open "what if" discussions without confusion.
» We discuss anything but same POR until we say "we change POR."

 The new teammate needs community to feel accepted and safe. Sometimes egos lead to an over-reach; a "grab-for-the-wheel" or an "I'm the leader" moment, usually with a blank page restart of some sort.

## 2.3.11 Handling Individual Contributions with Care and Respect

There is a right way and a wrong way to process and respond to the work of remote individuals.

### The wrong way:

- An individual contributes something to the team (code, whitepaper, business report, marketing content, whatever) and gets no response.

When remote team members send work for review, approval, or simple collaboration and nothing comes back, the work goes unrecognized and unread, it is valueless.

That work was assigned and should be recognized. If not, it's demotivating to the person who did the work. And it begs the question, why was the work assigned in the first place? Is the work valuable if it doesn't even merit the time to read it?

When this happens, it is clearly a failure *on the part of the team leader.* Don't fail your people. As team lead you gave them direction, you allocated company resources, they invested time and effort into completing the work.

### The right way:

- If the work is satisfactory, respond! "I read the note. Nice work, let's call this complete. Kindly post on team file share. And declare victory on your weekly. Hurray!!!"
- If the work merits a team review: "Nice work; if you feel this is ready for a team review, we can add to an upcoming agenda. How much time should we allocate?"
- If the work needs love: "Good progress, but needs a bit more love . . . a little more of "X," a little less of "Y," and please think about adding a call to action. If you need to discuss or need help, just ask. Thanks for the hard work, if it wasn't important it would not have been asked of you."

---

**GOOD PRACTICES**

- » Recognizing that the work creates connectedness. Ignoring the work implies it's valueless.
- » Recognize the work of everyone: every piece, every time, no exceptions.
- » If work is presented and it is outside of scope or schedule or resources, capture the work in the roadmap for consideration for the next version.

## 2.3.12 Navigating "Tech" vs. "Non-Tech," Liberal Arts vs. Math

There is a well-known communications gap between technical folks and non-technical folks. It's a problem, but fortunately there is an easy remedy.

- Tech folks have a tendency to dive right into the detail; this is off-putting for non-tech people.
- Non-tech folks frequently think and speak in terms that lack clarity to tech people; this is off-putting for tech people. Tech folks are listening for the specifics of the problem they are to solve, what they are to build, and why it will be both valuable and widely used.
- The remedy is to always start with a clear statement of the problem we will solve together—the thing both non-tech and tech can fully, and eagerly, understand.
- State the problem in terms of the customer pain you will relieve and the key success criteria.

Engineers solve problems: state the problem, get out of the way.

- Our right brain specializes in recognizing shapes, patterns, values, and motion and visualizes them in space and time.
- Our left brain specializes in language: grammar, vocabulary, speech comprehension, and social skills. Anecdotally, if you are searching for a word, look right, this stimulates the left side of the brain.

That said, we are all uniquely wired—these are shades-of-gray preferential topics. If someone happens to be good at math, they may still be good at creative writing, and vice versa. Assume the positive about people and their skills. Most of us dislike being typecast, and we react well to expanded roles, provided they don't trigger our fear of failure wiring. Good team leads will seek opportunities for teammates to contribute outside their normal range, outside their comfort zone. It will be rewarding to them. It will grow team experience and knowledge. And the results will often surprise.

## 2.3.13 Team Formation, Bias, and Business Consequences

We are wired for bias—and bias is *not OK*. It takes conscious and consistent effort to overcome.

We are wired to quickly (thoughtlessly) categorize. This is a result of thousands of generations of evolution: predator or prey, friend or foe. When people don't look like us or sound like us, our lizard brains categorize those people as "them."

The business consequence of bias disallows our organizations to take full advantage of global talent pools. We subconsciously assign the better tasks to "us" and the less desirable work to "them." Now, close your eyes for 60 seconds, imagine yourself on the receiving end of bias, a lifetime of constant bias: harder work, more risk, less reward. Bias is not OK for anyone involved. Bias does a disservice to them, to you, and to your organization.

Fortunately, we can overcome bias with objective logical thinking, rather than subjective categorization. When our projects are results based and measurable, we can objectively create a less biased, more merit-based workplace.

*When assigning tasks and projects, do so on merit.* When assessing raises and promotions, do so on merit. With tech projects based on specific goals, this is very feasible. In addition, it is possible to assign some of the "crappy" tasks to everyone, and assign some of the "choice" assignments to everyone (of course, accounting for skill).

The thing to avoid is assigning only "crappy" or no-win tasks only to those who are different than us. I have personally witnessed individuals set up for failure—bad karma.

## 2.3.14 Mind the "Tech" and "Non-Tech" Gap

Team-member-to-team-member communications and collaboration isn't instant. It will take a minute. As team lead, be prepared to do some coaching for non-tech folks. By example, walk them through a good problem statement. Show them how to avoid dictated solutions. Encourage them to capture the voice of the customer, the voice of the partner, the voice of the market, competitive dynamics—in writing. Encourage them to do peer review, page turners, just as you encourage tech peer reviews. This way, everyone learns. Watch out for any behavior in which something is "thrown over a wall" without a healthy two-way conversation.

As team lead, be prepared to do some coaching for the tech folks. By example, walk them through a use case, a sales cycle, a customer on-boarding, a quarterly business review. These walkthroughs will create understanding and empathy. Encourage tech folks to *start every conversation by describing the customer problem being addressed.* This is the best way to build a high-value working relationship between tech and non-tech.

Stick to clear problem statements and avoid dictated decisions. In their own lane, tech folks are subject matter experts: they've invested years in becoming masters. Given a bit of whitespace, masters will deliver an innovative, useful result, often doing more and often exceeding expectations. Dictating any solution negates that mastery, and engineers/tech individuals will respond negatively.

Tech topics are often complex and difficult to explain—especially, work in progress. Engineers can be mentally distracted with complex topics—it's unfair to see self-absorption and interpret that as rudeness, impatience, or abrasiveness. Truly, it's most likely their brain is elsewhere.

Tech folks and engineers don't like being told they are wrong: expect a negative emotional response. Of course, everyone on the team will try to overcome difficulties on their own, but make it team policy to ask for help when needed.

This is business, not school, where individual accomplishments are graded and valued. Rather, the value to our organization is based on results, and it takes both tech and non-tech working together to accomplish results.

**GOOD PRACTICES**

> » Team results matter. Each of us contributes something necessary and different to the project. The collaboration of teammates leads to results. Tech alone doesn't get results. Business alone doesn't get results.

 Our brains yearn for our community—a sense of purpose and place. These human needs are fulfilled with a clear vision of success and co-workers who collaborate to accomplish our shared team goals.

## 2.3.15 Team Interaction Is the Main Event, Not an Afterthought

We all get busy. Often, we are heads down on a specific task. Sometimes we get chronically busy. Don't allow your team to be low on your priority list. Just saying, "I trust you," does not create connections or belonging.

- If you are chronically busy, just set calendar time to "respond to team"; be diligent—your team merits your time.
- Tell them what to expect (and why): "For the next week I will be heads down on X. Don't let this hold you up, it's fine to proceed in my absence."
- Give your team autonomy. In most situations they can/should proceed without your input. They can organize peer reviews themselves—peer reviews keep them connected.
- Make your team your priority—their work matters. Consistently responding to your team keeps them connected and valued.
- Your team is more important than whatever shiny object crosses your desk.

This topic is important for remote teams, because individuals will already feel disconnected simply by being remote. It's our job as team leaders to overcompensate by giving recognition and clear feedback to every piece of work (every piece, period, no exceptions).

And a gentle reminder: there are always other uses for your team's time. They may do other gainful tasks for the business, or they may be doing other gainful tasks for some other employer. Ignoring work implies it's valueless, leading to diminished motivation, diminished contribution, and often attrition.

## 2.3.16 Team Lead Responsibility, Accountability

- **Bad news:** The team lead reports bad news and accepts accountability, publicly owns it, and makes it better.
- **Good news:** The team members responsible report good news—they deserve the credit.

Team leader avoids *anything* resembling taking credit for the hard work of others. This builds trust, builds your team, builds your community. The unacceptable alternative is be a "take the credit" leader, and a "lay the blame" leader.

This approach serves no one. It does not serve teammates: who would want to be on that team? Your talent will leave. It does not serve the organization, as it punishes initiative. It is a talent repellent. It does not even serve the leader, because that leader will eventually fail.

### Personal Lesson on Leader Accountability

I once inherited a dysfunctional remote devops team. We had immediate problems: one developer wrote code; he was remote and didn't have access to internal systems. Another person was responsible for testing; he had access to internal systems, but couldn't be bothered with versions, couldn't be bothered to test the right builds or give useful feedback to the developer. Every conversation was an exercise in passive resistance. Extremely frustrating.

I could have found fault with both the developer and the tester. I could have rightfully said "grow up and work together." And I was an inch away from making that serious mistake.

But, fortunately, I said instead: "I thought about this and looked in the mirror and realized I should have done a better job with goals and communications—my bad." I made a conscious effort to avoid placing individual blame for a team thing.

And so, together we looked at a devops wiki in which I had written the goals. We went around the table and clarified what we were testing and how to log results against a changing code base against a variety of hardware.

In reality, the devops problem wasn't simple, and it affected everyone. I could have (again) found fault with them, but I chose not to be negative or accusatory.

The result was the team had less passive resistance, and surprise! We successfully delivered on that project.

In truth, we can always do a better job on goals, communications, and dependability.

Dependability is your secret weapon, *be sure to do what you agreed to do.* It may involve nudging an individual or two. Team leader failure to follow through erodes results now and in the future.

Once this behavior of accountability has been demonstrated, encourage other team members to do the same.

◊ Team leader accepts accountability.
◊ Team leader isn't looking to place blame.
It's only about team results. Team leader is accountable for bad news and we are in a safe community.
Team members report good news, we are in a safe community.
◊ Team leader doesn't attempt to take credit for others' work.
◊ Team members report good news to leadership.
Exposure to leadership makes team members visible and valued—especially relevant with remote teams.
Connects leadership to employees—relevant for remote situations.

**GOOD PRACTICES**

» Lead the conversation to resolve an area of conflict or disagreement.
» Team leader assumes accountability—"I can do better"—and acknowledges they are less than perfect.
» "I looked in the mirror and realized I could have done a better job with goals and objectives."
» Let's review where we are and how we can work more efficiently.
» Humor helps, because working efficiently is waaayyy better than the alternative.

## 2.3.17 Soft Skills for the Tech Workplace

In any workplace, it's too easy to treat each other as disposable. Each of us is unique. And we each have different worldviews, different aspirations, different fears, different pressures and priorities within the workplace, and different priorities outside the workplace. Misaligned goals will lead to chronic conflict and passive resistance, frequently leading to departure of highly talented people and lower value, less talented people staying—and a vicious cycle begins.

In tech workplaces, the scenario is magnified by difficult-to-understand innovations, mismatch of business and tech goals, and strong personalities often encountered in engineering/tech teams.

Creating serial successes involves managing risk and delivery. Fortunately, there are ways to resolve conflicts swiftly and without tears. Shared goals and a clear plan of record is a very powerful tool to bring teams together. Further, the POR actually encourages healthy debate. The team can discuss alternative pros and cons. And at the end of the discussion, we can say, "Same POR," or, "We made the decision to change the POR." The POR may sound rigid, but it is a soft skill when it allows debate of alternatives, without leaving anyone confused. Once we resolve the confusion about what's needed, it's down to working together to get it done.

This all sums up to helping each other to achieve team goals and individual successes. It's simple empathy and willingness to help others. When we help others, we get personal satisfaction. When we allow others to help us, we know people care, are willing to help, and we are not alone.

## Lessons from Parenting (Without Tears)

"Fridge rules": When our children were small, my wife and I had a list of six rules, with consequences, on the refrigerator.

Children (well, mostly) like structure, clear boundaries, and consistency. When our children tested the boundaries, they would be ushered to the refrigerator, the rules would be read, and we had a "We are clear, yes?" moment. No punishments, and no tears.

Remote team conflict is not unlike parent–child or sibling–sibling conflict. If that conflict becomes chronic, everyone gets stressed. Negativity is a burden—similar to running a race wearing a backpack. The burden of negativity and negative self-talk spills over into other areas such as scholastics, participation in sports, theater, debate, community service, and music. These burdens can be resolved with the right handling.

The team lead carries the clear and unshared responsibility to build "team accountability"—where success equals team success, rather than individual success. And just like "fridge rules," keeping team goals and measurable success criteria front and center yields clear and consistent structure and serves to resolve, rather than create, conflict.

There will be disagreements, and there are healthy objective ways to disagree. The team lead ensures that disagreements get safely surfaced, objectively debated, and safely resolved. Disagreements can be raised objectively by relating problems to team goals (not relating problems to people or laying blame).

Our context for problems is always how they relate to shared team goals. Problems can be resolved without criticism, hurt feelings, or stimulating our negative brain wiring. When properly handled, problems are not allowed to become chronic disagreements or to chronically linger unresolved.

The team lead should encourage healthy discussions and debate of pros and cons. Debate is good when it's objective. Keeping debate focused on shared team goals makes the debate productive.

Catch your team doing something right. Recognize contributions. As discussions will surface about needed improvements of the team goals or updates to plan of record, improve the plan, in writing.

Your team influences the plan for the better, and that's great for all involved. The teammates get heard, they make a difference, it's good for them.

Add to the agenda for the team call. Review the improved plan with the team, and thank them for making the project a better one. And as other teammates observe, they will imitate and contribute, too. It's good for their morale, good for their career, good for their teammates, and good for the organization.

For remote teams, these same principles in clarity and consistency apply. We like structure (well, we dislike uncertainty and chaos); we like knowing our place in the community, we like knowing we are not alone.

## Finding Fault or Laying Blame on Individuals Rarely Works

Negative wiring related to bad news is magnified with isolated/remote team members. We are wired to magnify bad news:

- **Bad news:** There is a tiger over the north hill. Deal with that *right now*!
- **Good news:** There are berries over the south hill. Deal with that later.

Our ancient ancestors survived and passed that negative wiring on to us. When individuals get criticized, even when well intentioned, it triggers a primitive "unsafe," or fight-or-flight response, which only serves to shut down the parts of our brains used for reasoning and logic.

In addition, fight-or-flight neurological responses stimulate our short-term memory centers. So, they occupy a magnified place in our short-term and long-term memories—and that memory is tied (forever) to the person or people delivering that criticism.

Therefore, the answer is to accept accountability and make it about your leadership or the team, not about individuals. Making criticism about individuals creates long-lived passive resistance, which drags everything down.

UNSAFE!!!
  ◊  I am accused of failing. UNSAFE!!!
  ◊  My livelihood and insurance are threatened.
  ◊  Fight or flight response.
  ◊  Stop reasoning.
Amygdala controls fear emotion, overrides other parts of the brain; hypothalamus issues anatomical response.

## The Need for One-to-One Meetings, Early and Often

Projects have their honeymoon periods. It's a good idea to do one-to-one calls as the team engages in formation. It's a simple dialogue:

- "Are you OK with your role? Feeling set up for success? Adequate to do your work?"
- "Any blockers? Anything you need?"
- "Are you OK with our direction as a team?"
- "Anything the team needs? Future topics to work through?"

Take a breath, let your teammate speak. You should not feel the need to respond to each and every point. It is OK for you to say, "Let me think about it," and feel free to revisit.

Post-honeymoon, the hard work is underway. There are the usual difficulties: things don't happen as quickly or easily as they should. There are the usual personality difficulties. Fatigue sets in, and energy levels sag. Team leaders get busy too. This is the time when one-to-one calls are critical.

Same conversation as above: "How are you?," "How is the team?." This confirms to the teammate: you are important, your input matters, your role matters, and you matter. If left unattended, the teammates' survival wiring will kick in and they will assume the negative, and this is magnified when remote and separated from their community.

## Walking Meetings

https://www.tedeytan.com/2016/11/23/20546
https://hbr.org/2015/08/how-to-do-walking-meetings-right

## Flow

"In a flow state" (aka, "in the zone") is a recognized concept in psychology and occupational therapy.

A real-world example: While managing a development team, I had a superstar, James. James was all about Linux®, and not a fan of Microsoft NT. The team was tasked to port a Linux product to NT. I asked James to take a look at it and give an informed estimate of time and resources. I mentioned "I know NT isn't your wheelhouse or your passion. But please do the best you can, let me know if you need help."

His first report back: "This doesn't look good, I am thinking four to six months"

Next report: "Not as bad as I thought, likely four to six weeks"

Next report: "I got into the zone over the weekend, the port is done."

I am happy for James, and I am happy for our employer.

When we are in a flow state, time disappears, we are fully immersed, focused, and enjoying the task or activity. When we are in a flow state, our brains are so totally engaged, there is no brain power left for anything else.

Mihaly Csikszentmihalyi is a pioneer in the psychology of "flow."[5] He researched why artists and the like get absorbed in their work. He posited (and I agree) that our brains have a limited ability to multitask. Specifically, in this state there is no room for anything negative; only complete absorption in the task at hand. These summarize Mr. Csikszentmihalyi's thoughts about focus:

- Being completely involved with intense concentration, inner clarity
- Working on something worthwhile
- Knowing the activity is doable, you are in control
- Feeling part of something larger
- Serenity, beyond ourselves, beyond our egos
- Intrinsic motivation, the task is its own reward

According to Mr. Csikszentmihalyi, the *enemies* of flow are

- Worry
- Apathy
- Anxiety *[my note: being set up for failure]*
- Boredom
- Multi-tasking and chronic interruptions
- Tasks not worthwhile *[my note: unimportant or low-value projects]*

Great info, highly consistent with this study. Now, what to do with it? As we apply Mr. Csikszentmihalyi's insights into remote teams, we recognize that we are more able to get into the zone when our task is worthwhile, when

---

5  https://www.ted.com/talks/mihaly_csikszentmihalyi_flow_the_secret_to_happiness | https://en.wikipedia.org/wiki/Flow_(psychology)

our task is enjoyable, and when our minds are undistracted by negatives. We recognize the need to find belonging and becoming, and we recognize the need to avoid hitting the surviving button (which is often in the way when we are remote).

In our teams, we can ask individuals who they are and how they'd like to contribute to the project. Wherever possible, play your team to their strengths, task them to things they want to do.

In team meetings, we can ask about getting into the zone, make it a thing to strive for when we can. And it's possible to find flow even in the tasks we don't much like (as with James and NT).

### Empathy and Team Formation

Early in my career, I was tasked with all sorts of random, weird, short-fused things. When I was introduced to a new team, I learned the habit of doing something for others before asking others to do something for me. It's a simple gesture, that says, "You matter." Our sense of belonging is strengthened with each and every "you matter" moment. It is *not* a given that team formation fulfills these basic human social needs.

Teams *can* fulfill everyone's *need for purpose* and everyone's *need for a place.* These needs are consistent with our belong-and-become wiring. With new teams, especially when remote, our survival wiring can over-ride our belong-and-become wiring. The way to overcome our unhappy survival wiring, and stimulate our happy belong-and-become wiring, is simply to help each other in some small way. Empathy matters. Empathy is a choice. Empathy is only real if it is consistent and lasting.

## 2.4  Trail Map and Conclusion

- Tools are just tools. How teams use them to establish, work together, and accomplish significant goals is more important than tool minutiæ. Teams don't live by Zoom alone. To be consistently effective, remote tech teams need tools, but teams require nurturing.
- Define outcomes in terms of problem statements, not dictated solutions. Involve the team to find the ideal solution. Be clear about the goals and outcomes.
- Use the POR to stay focused—"We can discuss anything."
- Close every discussion with a clarifying statement: *"we did (or did not) change the POR."*
- Don't allow ignoring/re-imagining of the goals, outcomes or POR, as that's a disservice to others on the team.

- Short projects = successful projects. When new stuff is requested, push it into the next project rather than interrupt the current active project. Relentless prioritization is good for business.
- Engage the team for risk management. Stuff can go wrong, let's get ahead of it and either change the plan to avoid the risk *or* accept the risk together.
- Engage functional managers early and often, to confirm resources don't evaporate without forewarning.
- Play people to their strengths: ask simple questions (how would you prefer to contribute?)
- Is this assignment too easy or too challenging? Do you understand what's needed? Are you set up for success?
- Use your position as team lead to manage conflict: "I let the team down, I wasn't clear about the goals, let's revisit them." Don't lay blame, learn and improve.
- Insist on empathy and mutual respect.
- Ignoring input, not responding to reasonable requests needs to be (gently) addressed.
- Be vigilant to help "outsiders" contribute their very best work. Outsiders are frequently treated as second-class citizens, give them a voice and equal status as a team member. Outsiders are those not located at headquarters, those who speak English as a second language, and contractors not directly employed.
- Bring out the best in others and in yourself. None of us is afraid of hard work, we just need a bit of structure and to be set up for success.
- We are wired to find our place and our purpose.

Let's do that, because this is the way to functional remote teams.

# Chapter 3

## Day-to-Day Remote Teams

Let's begin with a sports metaphor. You just joined soccer team. The team is promising, but other teams are also promising and very competitive.

You and your teammates have improved, and you continue to improve, your skills over the months and years. Your team practices together diligently for months, all in the interest of playing well and winning as a team. There is also primitive brain wiring at play—the team becomes the community. Your (and their) tone of voice, facial expressions, and body language matters.

Although many sports teams enjoy healthy chemistry, not all do. There can be friction, beyond healthy competition, over who gets what position, playing time, money. It is not always sweetness and light. And consistent success (winning) is not about individual star players, it's about how all the players are committed to playing together to achieve success together. We are seeking commitment to the team.

*The key ingredient in building an effective team is determination, driven by shared will, to learn and improve.* This doesn't happen on day one. It takes continuous attention, effort, and focus on specific improvements. And just like sports teams, building a winning tech team takes time.

This section sets the tone of *continuous improvement and continuous learning.* These ingredients, along with shared goals and team results, are the things that heal team friction.

## 3.1 Running Meetings: Agenda Three-ish Topics

Stick to a short list of topics; first do a thorough job with the high-priority stuff. Keep the list short in the interest of having adequate time to do a thorough job—team discussions always take a bit more time than imagined. If you, the team lead, are doing all the talking, then you are doing it wrong.

Let everyone have a say; don't cut them off until they start covering old ground or repeating themselves. If they're covering old ground, politely direct them to the plan of record (POR) or past notes and move on. If they are upset, talk to them one on one later and discuss root cause and corrective action. Make sure the issue is cleared up and the team member is back on track.

During meetings, capture actions—what gets measured gets done. Actions have deliverables, owners; review actions from previous meeting actions to be short term. Put longer-term actions into the project plan. If the action is unwieldy, break it into several smaller, manageable actions. Consistently attempt to connect smaller captured actions to big picture desired outcomes.

This is so important for remote teams, because it's too easy for remote people to mentally check out. Involving them in dialogue, focusing on specifics, and capturing and following up on action items creates engagement, just like your favorite teachers did who were skilled at using questions and dialogue to keep everyone in class involved and focused.

### 3.1.1 "Around the Table" Meeting

I've had a long career; I have worked with hundreds of different people in leadership roles. This "go around the table" meeting is in my top favorites.

Our exec, Jim, would call a meeting. He would say, "Today, we are going to discuss . . . [topic]."

Person by person, he would go around the table and ask, "What do you think?" Sometimes he'd go around the table more than once. At the end of the meeting, Jim would say, "OK, here is what we will do . . . [guidance, decision]"

The beauty of his system is:

- It's a two-way conversation, *before* decisions get made. Everyone gets heard; their input is taken seriously.
- A decision is made, and everyone hears exactly the same words.
- Everyone knows they are expected to work to that end *with their teammates*.

I use a variation for team meetings. We cover the agenda (two to three points). Next, I go around the table and ask each person, "Do you have anything to share with the team?" I ask participants for topics they'd like to work into upcoming agendas.

The meeting wraps up with a review of actions, next steps, and (if any) changes to the POR. If there is a problem identified during the meeting, follow up is assigned and entered on the next week's agenda.

- It's a two-way conversation. Everyone gets heard, their input is taken seriously.
- Knowing they will be called on, each participant is more engaged. This engagement tool is often used by good teachers, when they ask individuals to answer a question.
- As decisions are made, we say either, "this changes the POR" or "no change to the POR," and every one hears exactly the same words.
- Everyone knows who is doing what.

Empathy is important here—put yourself in the shoes of the contributor. Team calls are for the benefit of the team, not just the team lead.

---

People want their voice to be heard by their community. It creates a sense of value and belonging.

&#9826; Confirm with individual contributors, project team meetings and status reports are the top priority. "If there are competing priorities, let me know."

&#9826; Expect consistent attendance, "We need you," "If it wasn't important, we would not ask."

&#9826; Don't accept spotty attendance, address it first with individual contributor, and again with individual contributor, and then with manager.

&#9826; Ask individual if they are getting consistent priorities from all (meaning team leader and manager).

---

**GOOD PRACTICES**

- » What gets measured gets done. Capture action items, follow up on action items.
- » Keep actions list immediate, short, and manageable. Capture longer-term decisions and data in project plan.
- » Overdue action items are a strong indicator of project risk. When tasks are overdue, get help from other team members.

### 3.1.2 Scorecards and Effective Meetings

Scorecards focus us on measurable success criteria; they drive team participation and collaboration. Score cards can be reviewed frequently or infrequently. Partner scorecards are typically reviewed quarterly; they are intended to provide clear and actionable feedback for both teams and partners to work going forward.

At their best, scorecards are crystal clear, focused on measurable outcomes, focused on key success criteria, and focused on the customer. Not all outcomes are of equal importance—balanced score cards clarify and weigh conflicting objectives and success criteria.

#### Table 3.1 Example Score Card

| Project Scorecard Dec 202x | Goal, Measurable | Comment | Score 1–7 | Weight 1–7 |
|---|---|---|---|---|
| Customer adoption | Increase from baseline 23% to 30% by Y-E | At start of q – 23% At end of q – 25% | 5 | 5 |
| Customer feedback | Improve Survey results from 73% positive to 77% positive | At start of q – 73% At end of q – 73% | 4 | 3 |
| Adjacent market adoption | Demonstrate adoption in XYZ market by 10% | At start of q – 0% At end of q – 0% | 4 | 1 |
| Competitive | Survey show preference over competitor by 10% | At start of q – us 23%, them 23% At end of q – us 25%, them 23% | 5 | 2 |
|  |  |  | 47/77 |  |

When we all know this is coming, we take extra effort to show progress.

Use scorecards for anything: team productivity, team unity, mentoring, customer feedback. Create scorecards as a group, so everyone knows what's important. Set team up for success with a high value/achievable stated outcome, and give everyone some whitespace to work with.

The act of creating a scorecard as a team is healthy; it increases engagement and buy-in, it shows everyone has an equal voice. Suggest doing this over a couple of iterations, get started, then refine/prioritize, then identify and manage risk. Call it done as part of the POR. See Figure 3.1 for sample scorecard.

| Scorecard "DOs" | Scorecard "DO NOTs" |
|---|---|
| • Scorecards focus us on the important.<br>• Keep it simple, no more than four items.<br>• Use several different scorecards for several different tasks—tech, quality, teamwork, business.<br>• Make sure scorecard is aligned with the POR. | • Don't make the scorecard too complex.<br>• Don't attempt to replace the project plan with scorecards.<br>• Don't allow the scorecard to conflict with the POR. |

**Figure 3.1**    Sample Scorecard

## 3.2 Overcoming Zoom-Out

Zoom® conference calls frequently suffer *Zoom-Out Syndrome*—when we stop engaging, stop caring, mentally check out after excessive Zoom meetings. Teams do not live by Zoom alone.

This is similar to project apathy but is magnified by being remote; lack of engagement is due to missing in-person presence. *This is easily cured by reenforcing, on a personal, one-on-one basis, that everyone needs a place and everyone needs a purpose.* The challenge is recognizing and being a positive, empathetic leader with effective one-on-one interactions.

Here are effective, one-on-one discussions to resolve Zoom-Out:

- Show concern and empathy—ask about work–life balance, exercise, time outside.
- Walking calls/meetings (esp. one on one): change of setting, time outside does a world of good. Simply lead by example.
- Review of project goals.
- Review how the individual fits into the overall goals.
- Confirm that the individual is being set up for success—having the will and the skill.
- Confirm that the individual is getting support from others on the team,
- Confirm that the project is set up for success (and the individual will share credit when that happens).

And in the team, without singling anyone out, talk about Zoom-Out, raise awareness, acknowledge that it happens to everyone (including team leads) to some degree. It's OK to be self-deprecating and say you experience Zoom-Out and are consciously countering it.

### 3.2.1 Video Conferencing, Screen Sharing, File Sharing, Scheduling Assistant Chat

Here is a prime example of multimodal learning: A while back, I had a very, very, very dry book I needed to read. I found that Microsoft Edge can *display* a PDF and *read it aloud* to you—multimodal learning. I finished the book, and my understanding and recall of the content was better than expected.

Multimodal learning applies to video calls. When we engage on a video call, we hear the voice and we see the expressions and the body language. Our primitive brains pick up on gestures, facial expressions, tone of voice. Video conferencing offers all these things, and is definitely worth the extra effort to use.

Create a norm that team meetings use video, so everyone sees everyone. The reason is that expressions and body language re-enforce the spoken word.

---

◊ Use video calls, *every time.*
◊ Multimodal (multiple senses: hearing and seeing) learning is improved. Faces matter for learning, and faces are a must to form the "community."
◊ Use VIDEO to fully engage (tone of voice, body language, facial expressions). This encourages more offline methods to engage (such as chat).
◊ One-on-one chat increases engagement, in safety.

---

## 3.3 Status Reports

### Monitoring Progress—Speedometers Do Not Slow Cars

It's critically important that team members are *not* punished for participating in schedule management.

Carrots and sticks: the schedule is *not* a stick. Schedules are created and monitored to manage risk. This is about team success and team results. We use schedules to identify problems in order to have time to do something about them. When we see a task that shows no progress or is overdue, someone needs some help. Get them help.

Weekly report: every task has a beginning and an ending. Keep the task names consistent, report 0%, 25%, 50%, 75%, or 100%. Keep the task list short to what's in progress. No more than five-ish tasks, just the priorities and immediate work. Anything more than that may be too many.

**Table 3.2  Jane Doe – weekly – mm dd yyyy**

| task 21 | 0% | | |
|---|---|---|---|
| task 32 | 25% | | |
| task 43 | 100% | | |
| Comment:<br>Next week start on task 21<br>Next week lead/organize a code review of task 43<br>Next week participate in code review of task 11<br>Self-training—functional programming software patterns and unit test | | | |
| Blockers:<br>Need a review of unit test | | | |

Comments are optional, blockers are optional. Getting hung up and asking for help is OK. Getting hung up and not asking for help isn't OK.

A sample weekly report can be seen in Table 3.2. This example is "software-ish," and it works equally well for content, marketing, operations, or sales.

Sometimes things take longer than expected—that's life. Lingering tasks are a clear indicator of project risk. The team leader looks for items that have started but are without progress for several weeks; the lead asks "Team Member A" if help is needed or suggests that a senior team member give help.

At all costs, avoid tying negative baggage to getting hung up and getting help. This is 100% about team success, and resolving blockers is the right way to achieve stated goals and key success criteria.

The act of giving help is its own reward—helps us feel part of something bigger. The tougher half of this conversation is asking for help. We are trained to do it ourselves and asking for help is a negative.

When offering help, I usually say, "Lots of people helped me in my early career, I am simply following their good example. I know you will help others when the opportunity presents." This serves to say, "You have a place, a purpose, larger than just yourself."

### 3.3.1  Real-World Schedule Monitoring and Recovery

Team lead notices that a specific task has shown 25% for two weekly reports. Team lead says to Team Member B (senior tech team member):

- "This task looks like it's stalled. Can you give Team Member A some help?"
- "This is not a criticism of A, they simply look hung up on this one little thing. No need to throw anyone under the bus."

Yes, this exact thing happened on one of my projects. B helped A, who wasn't criticized in any way. The project execution was on schedule, on scope, on quality, on budget. Team success, no individual blame or individual credit.

---

**GOOD PRACTICES**

- » Risk management is to identify/avoid problems.
- » Schedule monitoring is risk management during the project—find out about problems in time to do something about them.
- » Dictated schedule is a big risk, no schedule is a big risk. Schedule without monitoring is a big risk.
- » Asking for help is a good thing. Refusing help is not good for the team.

---

◊ My contributions matter. I can show my contribution, I show my progress, there is no drama.
◊ This team leader isn't micromanaging, finding fault, or laying blame.
◊ This team leader doesn't lie or tell half-truths.
◊ This team leader is going for team success (period).

---

**GOOD PRACTICES**

- » In your real-world team, identify a blocker and discuss it. Ask about root cause, ask about corrective actions.
- » Assign a pair to work the problem. Be assertive. It's the team leader's job to resolve those blockers. Provide help where help is needed.
- » Follow up offline, follow up on team call to show resolution.

## 3.3.2 Getting and Giving Help as a Way to Reduce, Resolve Conflict

Getting and giving help keeps us connected. *Getting and giving help is good for morale.*

There is healthy brain chemistry associated with helping, teaching, and interacting with others. Multiple scientific surveys confirm that we are happier giving to others than spending money on ourselves. To me, this shouts community wiring, the need to belong.

Encourage everyone to ask for help. It's healthy and everyone learns: the person getting the help, the person giving the help, the team—we all benefit.

Be assertive and assign the person to provide the help. Don't be shy, it's the team leader's job to resolve those blockers and keep the project moving forward smoothly.

An additional nuance: assign two people to resolve friction between team members. If it appears Team Member A and Team Member B are having friction, assign Team Member B to help Team Member A. Follow up offline, give it love and attention.

Assume the positive: "Hi A, hi B, just checking in, not pushing, just asking . . . I trust you are making progress on that blocker. Please let me know what to expect. If it wasn't important, I wouldn't ask."

---

**GOOD PRACTICES**

During team call, confirm this issue is resolved, showing the closure is healthy, shows progress, shows teams work, and gives confidence to other team members.

## 3.4 Blockers

Consistent discussion of blockers is both offense and defense.

- **Offense:** Focus the team on results; discussing and removing blockers communicates that results matter.
- **Defense:** For teams, or for individuals, if there needs to be a frank discussion of performance problems, that conversation can proceed without pointing or excuses. Clear and consistent statement of goals and success criteria and consistent discussion and removal of blockers allow a "no excuses" discussion. Anything less suggests a failure of leadership.

Ask about blockers in both team meetings and one-on-one meetings. Resolving blockers is the best way to get the best results from your team.

◊ Discussion of blockers means leaders are setting the team up for success. This improves our belonging instinct, as we work as a team toward clear goals. This improves our becoming instinct as we accomplish our goals.

◊ If leaders don't address blockers, we often perceive we are being set up for failure. Our survival instinct then kicks in, reducing our ability to think logically, reducing our ability to work with others smoothly, and significantly reducing our ability to perform with clarity and confidence.

---

> » During team calls, always ask about blockers. During one-on-one calls, always ask about blockers.

## 3.5 We Made a Mistake, What Did We Learn?

Tech projects are hard. Mistakes and obstacles are a reality. Unhealthy teams allow problems to go uncorrected, and then problems become chronic. But that's an uncomfortable conversation; we don't like being told we are wrong. It's even worse to be told we are wrong in front of our team (our "tribe"). The art in this situation is to make it about the team and avoid making it about the individual. This triggers the good instinct-to-become wiring and avoids triggering the bad instinct-to-survive wiring, which diminishes our ability to think logically.

Good team leaders and healthy teams learn and improve. This means acknowledging mistakes. Healthy teams call out problems in the context of relevance to team and goals and results. This is what that might sound like:

- "Hi team, we didn't have a great week, let's take a minute to review, learn, and improve."
- "As I thought about the situation and considered my role, *I recognize I could have done a better job* of clarifying and communicating our goals. My bad, I will work to improve this area. Your feedback is welcome and encouraged."
- "We hit Obstacle 1, Obstacle 2. Is that correct? Any clarification, additional detail?"
- "What are root causes and corrective actions for 1 and 2?"
- "To learn or improve, I suggest we do X and Y. Is that reasonable?"
- "OK, *we learn, we improve and we move on. The past is the past.* Just like a winning sports team, we need to practice and play together to perform better. Today we learned and got just little bit better as a team."

This approach avoids singling out individuals. It shows that the team lead is accountable and will not pass the blame. This approach keeps it objective, focuses on the problem and root cause without assigning blame. It serves to resolve problems and move forward into positive space. Positive space triggers our instinct-to-become frontal brain wiring. By avoiding dwelling on the negative, we avoid triggering our primitive survival brain wiring and diminishing our ability to think logically.

Consistency and follow up are essential. Do your best to identify and improve on each and every teachable moment. It's critical to avoid picking on one area while ignoring other areas. Avoid playing favorites, which will result in alienating part of the team.

This is a marathon, not a sprint. Consistency, determination, and kindness are the key ingredients. Golden rule stuff: is this the type of team you would like to be a part of?

## 3.6 During Meeting (If Conversation Isn't Resolving)

Debate is OK, and team leader should know when to be quiet and listen for point of diminishing returns. If the debate stalls, organize a single-topic meeting and break the action into smaller pieces. It's fine for single-topic meetings to be run by others; they need *not* be organized by team lead. Active dissent is OK. Disagree objectively, with facts that pertain to project goals.

Weighted scorecards are one way to lead the team through a structured review of what is more important and less important in a complex situation. Scorecards get people focused on the scorecard, rather than on each other.

Chronic arguments without resolution nearly always harm the entire effort and all involved. It is rarely OK to stall; if you disagree, say why objectively, with supporting data, view the alternatives objectively, and seek the supporting data. There comes a point when all must choose only one of several less-than-perfect plans, and all must commit to executing that selected plan. The leader has the responsibility to capture that plan in writing, within the POR.

 Everyone needs a place in which it's OK to speak up, but we all need to be prepared to win some and lose some. We don't win every debate, and sometimes we should go with the will of the community—"disagree and commit."

## 3.7 Fear and Accurate Data

W. Edwards Deming said in *The New Economics*[1]

> *Bearers of bad news fare badly. To keep his job, anyone may present to his boss only good news. Fear invites wrong figures.*

Following are the earmarks of dysfunction:

- Bad news is seen unfavorably by your organization.
- People reporting bad news are seen unfavorably by your organization.
- Your organization focuses on finding fault, and people focus on avoiding blame.

---

[1]  https://www.amazon.com/New-Economics-Industry-Government-Education/dp/0262541165

It will be no surprise that bad news ceases to be reported, and from there it's a downward spiral. Data is not collected, or is simply hidden. Every decision creates career risk, while no decision is OK. Execs are increasingly frustrated by lack of results. Executive counterproductive behavior is magnified when execs encounter any real issue. Usually mid-level managers pass the blame downhill to some unfortunate individuals who happen to be in the wrong place.

This leads to a state in which data is not reported or is misreported, and no continuous improvement happens.

The earmarks of effective remote teams are in fact exactly the opposite:

- Bad news is seen as an opportunity to learn, improve, and better manage risk.
- People reporting bad news are simply doing their job. It's about fixing the problem, not finding blame. if the problem is unknown or unclear, it will not be solved, and continuous improvement stalls.
- Your organization focuses on root cause and corrective action, then people can focus on the problem and the fix, not on avoiding blame.

This is a worthwhile pursuit to develop organizational capabilities and a competitive advantage: recruiting from anyplace, reduced office expenses, and lastly building reliable global resource capabilities for situations in which other full-time people are fully booked or have a skills gap.

---

**BEST KNOWN METHODS**

The remedy is very, very, simple.

» Team lets team leaders know about a problem in time to do something about it.
» Team leaders report bad news, accept accountability for bad news.
» Team leaders build relentless focus on fixing the issue, avoid laying blame on individuals.
» The team supports the team leader in identifying the remedy, and implementing the remedy before it impacts scope-schedule-resources.

# 3.8 Managing Information

Big picture clarity is a keystone of successful projects. Fortunately, information management just takes a bit of discipline.

- Capture project goals, review with the team, store on a wiki or similar.
- Capture project POR, review with the team, store on a wiki or similar, keep it current, and when POR changes let the team know.
- Capture devops or engineering process and risk management, review with the team, store on a wiki or similar.

- Capture engineering docs, review with the team, store on a wiki or similar.
- Capture what is out of scope and working plan for next revision, review with the team, store on a wiki or similar.
- Capture IT Rundeck®, user manuals, quality and support docs, review with the team, store on a wiki or similar.
- Capture sales and marketing materials, review with the team, store on a wiki or similar.
- Publish automated testing metrics, open/closed/deferred defects, and defect arrival/fix rates.

Keep projects small, avoid changing project fundamentals, otherwise they fail.

## 3.9 The Art (and the Need) for One-on-One Meetings

For remote teams, it is critical to make that personal connection. One-on-one, informal discussions lead to trust and openness for that future moment when that trust is truly needed.

Walking meetings are different because they have no barriers such as email, PowerPoint, or a physical desk between the two of you. Walking meetings have no authority-saturated settings, such as an executive office or a formal meeting room, to subconsciously communicate authority. Walking meetings dissolve these numerous differences in seniority.

Walking meetings do work on smart phones! First, outdoors is a mood lifter. Outdoors is good for the soul. Second, exercise is a mood lifter. Exercise is among our best, most under-used, antidepressants. Third, walking meetings invite participants to speak more about how they feel and what they think. This improves connectedness and engagement. Asking about morale says they matter to you and to the company.

Lastly, walking meetings are known to improve creativity, and the walking meeting setting improves a positive sharing experience, whereas a formal conference room reduces our collective appetites for sharing and collaborating.

If you must have an uncomfortable conversation about workplace behavior or bias, its complex, its often subconscious, it's always irrational. My approach (just one suggestion, and there are many other appropriate and effective ways of dealing with this). But this has worked for me. "What if English wasn't your first language? What if you didn't feel like you fit in? What if you weren't at headquarters with executive buddies?" "If you are in their situation, how would you want to be treated?"

This serves to create empathy; it isn't exactly an accusation (but it is implied). The conversation can be used to simply see the situation from another viewpoint.

## 3.10 Failure and Cross-Functional Teams

### True Story:

A peer program manager had gotten marching orders from execs to produce a server appliance for a specific IT inventory and support task. The program manager and the development team of 20 went away for six months. When they came back, the server appliance was ready to launch. The program manager got up in front of a room of salespeople, he did the brief, and asked for a show of hands, "Do your customers need this?" No hands went up—Ouch! Ten+ staff-years chasing a problem no one had!

This could have been avoided easily with an early-project effort to validate the concept—maybe a dozen phone calls. Definitely worth gathering the customer feedback (aka, user stories).

*We are confirming these IT inventory and support tasks are (or are NOT) significant problems and there are no viable alternative solutions.*

### Another True Story:

This is one of my efforts to uncover customer need (customer pain). When I was a product manager at WD (the disk drive company), I was asked to present to executive staff on a possible fibre channel (FC) disk drive. I found that only seven companies in the world consumed FC disk drives: EMC, Sun, HP, and similar. I called the proper individuals at each of these companies.

*Hi, for your systems using FC disk drives, we are aware you buy from Maxtor or Seagate. Do you need a third supplier?*

I had a nice chat with all seven, and made some new friends. Every one of them said, "No, we don't need another supplier."

When I presented to WD exec staff, here's how the conversation went:

Me: "Do you want the short answer or the long answer?"

Them: "That's a stupid question, we want the short answer."

Me: "There are seven buyers of FC drives. I called, and all seven said they had no need for a third FC supplier."

Them: "Good job, you can leave now."

My first WD executive briefing. Hurray!

The next week we collected voice of the customer related to hard disks for video surveillance; this was a significant, underserved market and turned out to be a real home run for WD. And that surveillance product line would not have been delivered if those resources were consumed working on a "not-needed" FC drive.

The digital economy causes us to constantly seek to be valuable and relevant. But, there will rarely be "universal appeal" to all people. Reality is that all people do not have the same problems, and therefore all people don't need the same solution.

Folksy wisdom: *Don't boil the ocean.*

This is where cross-functional teams come in, specifically to collect customer insights and user stories. In the absence of first-hand customer interaction, tech teams are just guessing. And fear of being wrong leads to attempts to identify some universal/ubiquitous project (aka, a boil-the-ocean project). Customer interactions relieve this project risk.

This is the reason cross-functional teams are essential. Sales and marketing's task in a cross-functional team is to identify unsatisfied or poorly addressed customer needs.

- Business/marketing/sales role is to navigate our shades-of-grey world.
- To find the poorly served groups of customers and delight those customers.

This serves to identify specific actionable problems and therefore avoid boiling the ocean.

Do a pre-meeting to structure questions to uncover customer need, customer pain, and make sure you are talking to the right customer person (GM/BU heads, rather than procurement/lower price folks).

Talk to the right people. The source of the voice of the customer is critical.

When you get feedback along the lines of "Company-X says they want . . . " or "Division-Y says they want . . . ," it's time to confirm the feedback originated from the proper human/role.

When capturing voice of the customer, also consistently capture the source organization and the source human/role within it. Anyone who manages profit/loss is a good candidate. Anyone saying "lower price is all we need" is likely in procurement and *not* a good source of voice of the customer. Anyone saying "tell me how it works" is likely in engineering and *not* a good source of voice of the customer. The right feedback from the right humans in the right role make the difference. Revisiting my WD experience above, what if I had asked the wrong people and they had mischaracterized the market need for FC drives? Without exaggeration, this single moment led to a massive shift in the HDD market (measured in $billions).

The right voice of the customer feeds our ability to work as a team, and feeds our instinct to instincts to become. Voice of the customer diminishes our perceived risk of being wrong (the trigger of our survival wiring). When customer pain is defined as problem statements (aka, agile user stories) rather than dictated solutions, then creativity and innovation become possible.

Creativity and innovation are key ingredients in our digital economy. Creativity and innovation are essentially risk taking. We present something creative or some innovation; it will be less than perfect, it will appeal to some and repel others; and black/white mindsets of right/wrong are simply contrary to the world we live in.

## 3.11 Sales Playbooks as a Team Tool

An important team exercise to navigate the customer question is building the sales playbook.

Sales playbooks are written for the use of sales/marketing and the like. This simple format has worked well for me over the years:

- The elevator pitch, the 20-minute slides
- What problem this solves, why it's better and different
- Listing of other satisfied customers
- Customer and personal profiles
- Q&A (thinly disguised objection handling)
- Where to go for help, what to do if there are problems

Doing this exercise as a team—early—clarifies who the customer is, what problems they have, what objections they may voice. But the biggest value is clarity and understanding of business and customer realities by the tech team. And if done early, this exercise surfaces things like support/trouble tickets/partners/knowledge exchange and will remedy post-delivery problems.

**BEST KNOWN METHODS**

Do a team exercise to draft the sales playbook, early in the project.

## 3.12 Empathy

*About you and your empathy*—empathy is a conscious choice. Being consistently empathetic takes focus and significant effort.

As a project moves along and fatigue sets in, we will find situations in which we don't want to accept the burden of hearing and attempting to improve.

- Consistent empathy is the only genuine form of empathy.
- Occasionally going through the motions of acting empathetic is not genuine.
- Your teammates will notice when you are not empathetic, and, either consciously or subconsciously, their desire to belong and become will diminish—and their wiring to survive will be stimulated more frequently.

I urge you to set your mind to being consistently empathetic, put your team first over the long haul. Your project benefits, your organization benefits, you benefit, and your teammates benefit. This is essential for career advancement for you and for your team.

You can consciously choose empathy, or choose narcissism. This is the among the most significant career choices you will ever make.

*About empathy in those around you*—it is worthwhile to consider the empathy of those around you, especially those above you in the organization. People are complex illogical beings and not easily decoded; with that said, I see executives fall into two very distinct types:

1. Those who genuinely want to be part of something bigger than themselves. Money is a secondary factor.
2. Those who are coin-operated, just in it for themselves. Money IS the over-riding factor.

To get this sorted, visualize a workplace absent of money and visualize a workplace where the task and the people are the reward. Imagine the new behavior of those around you.

- Would they have an appetite for the work? Genuinely?
- Would they work to improve their craft? Read? Take classes? Would they grow as professionals?
- Would they willingly take on tasks which benefit the team, but not themselves?
- Would they seek situations to work with others and help others in their careers?

When money is out of the equation, it's easy to know the folks who work to be part of something bigger; they have a purpose and a place. These are the folks you want to surround yourself with. Because those other folks, who are just in it for the money, sadly have a void in their place and their purpose, and are not worth the limited years in your career.

You can change you, you cannot (usually) change others.

 When you express empathy, you are communicating your care about the other person, you are treating that person as they are part of your tribe, part of your community. Everyone needs a place. Empathy builds community.

» Be consistent in showing empathy. Everyone has their ups and downs, their victories and their defeats.

» When work is too hard, it can be demoralizing. When work is consistently too easy, it can be demeaning. It's always reasonable to ask if work is too challenging or not challenging enough.

» Simply show you care about your co-workers as human beings trying to make the best of an imperfect world.

# 3.13 Trail Map and Conclusion

• Include everyone as much as possible. Around the table: "Jim, is there something you'd like to share with the team?"

• Managing a stable POR, disallow ignoring POR, disallow re-imagining of POR. Manage uncertainty with roadmaps.

• Scorecards: what gets measured gets done.

• "Building a solid team takes a time and effort. We don't expect it to be perfect. I am not perfect and don't expect you to be perfect either."

• "What did we learn?"

• "We had a rough week, what can we do to learn, improve?"

• Be relentless about disallowing bias.

• Weekly progress reports: task 1 100%, task 2 75%, task 3 50%, task 4 25%, task 5 0% done.

• Draft the playbook and the brochure as a team to drive shared understanding.

• Lead with empathy.

# Chapter 4

## Innovation and Uncertainty

The act of innovation (aka, creation, invention) is difficult. Innovation has been compared to "seeing the sausage being made."

> *We know from the history of Thomas Edison, innovation and creation are, at best, imperfect; and innovation, at its worst is a parade of failure, often highly visible. Edison failed 1,000+ times in his efforts to invent the lightbulb. These failures were visible to the people in his life, to his staff, his family, and his investors. This was the experience of Thomas Edison.*[1]

Let's recognize all the adjacent work Edison did to make the electric light practical and create a self-sustaining company (Edison General Electric) to grow the incandescent light first from an experiment, next to replace natural gas lighting, next to become a ubiquitous source of light everywhere. Adjacent work included inventing a better vacuum pump, electric meters, cables, generators, and (my favorite) variable resistors. These were all valuable skills, intellectual property, capabilities, and assets for Edison. And for your organization, the ability to efficiently produce digital assets—web content, web and brand presence, web-driven intelligence, digital customer interaction, and back office business operations logic—are valuable skills, intellectual property, capabilities, and assets for your organization.

---

[1] https://thomasedisonlight.weebly.com/funding.html

## 4.1 Innovation, Uncertainty, and Our Brains

*It is better to light one candle than to curse the darkness.*

— Chinese proverb

The point is, innovation is painful. But failing to attempt innovation is worse. Innovation involves uncertainty and often failure. Who among us is continuously motivated when efforts often end in failure or the inventor is perceived as a failure? Innovation is even more painful in workplaces in which failure is punished and successes go unrecognized and unrewarded (all stick and no carrot).

Visiting our primitive wiring, we are wired to assume bad news, "We saw a lion," over good news, "We saw edible berries." Which do you hear louder? We are wired to be skeptical (or even fear) what we don't understand. Our primitive minds say to us, "There might be a lion," and, "We don't know for sure there will be berries." Innovation is the unknown, and it's scary when we don't know all the answers.

Flash forward to the current day. Our primitive wiring gets involved when we face innovation tasks. We might fail, we might be wrong, and our status might suffer. When faced with uncertainty, it's too easy to indulge our primitive (mostly negative) wiring and stall progress with a string of negative assumptions.

- Do we know it will work? "It might not work."
- Do we know how long it will take? "What if it takes too long?"
- Do we know for sure customers will like it? "What if customers do not like it?"

The common thread is assuming the negative: "It might not [work, sell, etc.]."

### 4.1.1 Handling Uncertainty Day to Day

Debate is fine, but the conversation *must* resolve to the best possible plan in the face of the unknown. Even a list of "known unknowns" is useful, as they are actionable. We gather facts to either confirm or discharge our fears. Early in the project, when you hear negative self-talk, simply make it actionable.

*Do we feel strongly that we need to find some specific resolution? What are the consequences of inaction? Get the team thinking about the consequences of doing nothing.*

*". . . OK, thanks for voicing the concern, Bill. Since you are closest to the situation, can you lead a team discussion after a bit of research?" Action: Bill will clearly define the problem/risk, collect available data, check the facts, and prepare to discuss at the next team call—clear and actionable problem statements.*

Innovation-friendly organizations often also embrace the scientific process: theory–experiment–analyze–improve. They are OK with mistakes, it's part of the process. These innovation-friendly organizations reward the attempt, even when results fall short.

Innovation-hostile organizations operate like a factory: do what you are told, exactly; don't mess up, and you'll be fine. Many of these organizations have evolved to "no mistakes tolerated," wherein the only thing that matters is "don't mess up"—results don't matter. These places are holdovers from factory management hierarchies. Factory-type management is innovation hostile. Factory management hierarchies don't work for tech (period). The band-aid is a "cross-functional" team. And these can work, as long as the functional managers and related entourage stays away. But, regrettably the "no mistakes allowed" cultures force functional managers and entourage back into micromanagement.

When people outside the project inject themselves, the suggested response is:

- We trust the success criteria and outcomes are on target. Yes?
- But a review will benefit us both.
- So, no changes to success criteria or outcomes, correct?
- We will make sure the folks tasked to attain these outcomes get your input.

Mistakes fuel innovation. Mistakes are a mandatory part of the innovation process. When tech teams are tasked with innovation, it is critical to have leeway to make mistakes.

**BEST KNOWN METHODS**

» Focus on key success criteria, outcomes and high-level problem statements, customer stories/customer interaction.

» Avoid things that thwart innovation: factory hierarchy management, excessive executive "don't be wrong" decision making, excessive functional supervisor micromanagement, and heavy decision–approval processes.

» Celebrate mistakes where possible. When you encounter significant problems have the "what did we learn" conversation in a team meeting, and don't lay blame on individuals.

## 4.2 Managing Uncertainty with Roadmaps

Having a clear plan of record and a roadmap for subsequent releases is *the* method to avoid constantly changing requirements, as this avoids failed projects.

*Relevance to remote teams:* clear, unchanging requirements paint the picture of success in our minds. Projects fail when the requirements are poorly understood and/or keep changing. The remedy is to keep projects short, and when the inevitable requests for changes happen, the answer is:

*"We are only X weeks away from completing this phase. This request will go onto the roadmap and into a future release rather than disrupt this current release." Alternatively, add this new request as a separate project, like a plug-in or extension which does not disrupt this current release.*

## 4.2.1 The Role of Roadmaps

- Capture the plan of record (POR).
- Capture requests/concepts for next projects.
- Capture key success criteria, outcomes (aka, "power metrics").
- Capture what is outside of scope.
- Capture detailed specifications to frame customer problem without dictating solution.

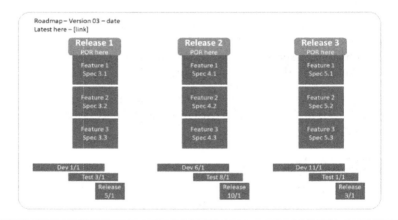

**Figure 4.1**    Roadmap Versions and Dates

Roadmaps change from time to time (see Figure 4.1). That's not a bad thing, because the whole point of a roadmap is shared goals and efficient team execution. Let's be working off the same plan. Always version/date the roadmap, always include a link to the online place at which the latest/current version can be found (SharePoint®, wiki, shared folder).

Every release will have its POR and a link to the latest version. Releases will have some target timeline with major milestones. Every release will organize a list of key features.

Every feature will include references to specifications, including key success criteria. Pointers to specs serves to avoid disconnects where roadmaps are shallow, ill-defined, ill-understood bullet points.

People outside the team can overlook the work already in plan. Often external people ask for immediate response, and when they do, discussing the new request in the context of a well-organized roadmap serves everyone well.

---

**BEST KNOWN METHODS**

Use roadmaps to maintain your march toward the bigger goals. Good ideas present themselves along the way. Some ideas will make the immediate release, some will need to be deferred. Use roadmaps to prioritize efforts to focus on the high-value, time-sensitive outcomes and capture good ideas to be worked later.

## 4.3 Remote Teams and Innovation

Successful innovation teams start by addressing an underserved market.

The Apple® Macintosh® tag line was "think differently." Macs were for the everyman, the underdog with great ideas aspiring to take on the world. This was the underserved market for the Mac.

During my time at WD, we found underserved markets in video surveillance, data backup/protection, and cloud email. They needed disk drives with both high capacity and reliability (i.e., not optimized for performance). These customers were underserved by large-capacity but unreliable desktop-class disk drives and by server drives which were both expensive and low capacity. Server drives were optimized for performance, not capacity. The WD Raid Edition was capacity optimized and reliable. The product line was a home run. It was not about technology; it was about the underserved market.

Customer validation is the starting point of innovation. Innovation should focus first on underserved customers and underserved markets to identify a targeted business pain to remedy. High-value and time-sensitive business problems are best. Competition is OK, that means there is a market. Imitation is not OK—your innovation must be different and better in some way. The most straightforward way to prime the pump of team innovation is customer feedback. This frames customer problems. This gets past the, "We don't know what to build" hurdle. This gets the entire team contributing.

We have a fear of being wrong and often opt for being silent over contributing content which might be less than perfect. The perfection mindset—"your work must be perfect"—leading to a "fear of imperfection" mindset is drilled into us in University.

In *any* team, we must work to overcome the perfection mindset. In *remote* teams, we must work harder to do so. People are shy, especially those of different cultures or different first languages. The job of the team leader is to coach them into contributing and feeling valued for contributing, even when contributions are less than perfect, even when some brainstorming doesn't make it into the project.

To initiate innovation at the team level for remote teams:

- We employ user stories and a stable POR focusing on problem statements and outcomes rather than dictated solutions.
- We use agile work structures, and when work is handed off, the team wins as they progress toward shared team goals.
- We do not micromanage, assign blame, or subjectively criticize individuals. We collaborate and innovate with the team through regular team calls with brainstorming time.

The bigger challenge is an organizational appetite for innovation. Lots of organizations will claim "we need to innovate," and in the same motion, innovation efforts will be underfunded, understaffed, get micromanaged, get outright interference from other parts of the company.

In half-hearted innovation efforts, typically, one or two people will be tasked to come up with innovations. The ideas are presented to executive staff. And no matter how good the technical materials, no matter how good the business justification, no matter how much pre-briefing, egos, and narcissism come into play, the proposals just die. This is no fault of the planning team or tech leadership; it is a failing of executive staff. Not all exec staffs are like that, but many are, I've seen it personally.

Thankfully, there are many examples of companies that have a real appetite for innovation and a real long-term view: Nvidia®, Microsoft®, Apple, WalMart®, World Wide Technology®.

In order for real innovation to happen, the organization needs to strive for full throated, enthusiastic innovation. These practices must prevail:

- Start with business analysis. Actively review and learn from case studies that contrast and compare successful innovators (Apple Mac v. IBM®-PC, WalMart v. K-Mart®, Nvidia® v. Sun Microsystems®). Then ask, "What happens if we do nothing or if we don't innovate?"
- Keep those business people allocated to the innovation cross-functional team. Avoid assigning two hours per week or low priority, as this is the equivalent of underfunding innovation.
- Use the scientific process and agile teams. Factory management hierarchies do not apply. Functional management, micromanagement, and matrix management do not apply.
- Adequately fund and staff innovation. In fact, overfund innovation, because mistakes and setbacks will happen. Allocate funding for innovation delivery.

## 4.4 Uncertainty of Data Science/AI/ML

*If data science was easy, then anyone could do it, right?*

Data science and AI present a unique challenge. In this era of digital transformation, data science and AI are essential, unlike typical IT projects, as they require experiment and discovery. Fortunately, data science, artificial intelligence, and machine learning are difficult, but not impossible.

Data science/AI/ML is a huge opportunity for tech professionals, as AI/ML is highly successful in certain situations (Google®, WalMart, Target®, National Labs). AI/ML has yet to turn the corner to mainstream business. The good news: there is a wealth of online training, and as business operations people engage with data scientists on business problems (aka, agile user stories for AI/ML), we will know mainstream adoption.

Today's challenge is that uncertainty is gating the pace of adoption of AI/ML. Data science is its own unique type of uncertainty.

Information technologies typically deal with observation. The data reflects what *has happened.* For example, we collect cash register transactions, or travel reservations, or sensor readings. We can observe that data as sorted by point in time, or sorted by the highest, or sorted by the lowest, or sorted by location. You get the idea: the data is captured then observed.

Data science typically deals with "correlation." The data reflects what *might happen*: statistical examination of the past as a predictor of what may happen in future similar situations.

- If a shopper buys towels, there is a high probability they will also buy bathroom mats.
- If a shopper buys diapers, there is a high probability they will also buy beer.
- If a music listener likes Alicia Keys, there is a low probability of the same listener also liking Black Sabbath.

But the value of these probabilities varies widely, based on a wide range of other variables. For the towel-buying example, warm climates near water will change the buying behavior. For the beer and diapers example, younger communities have more kids, diapers, and beer than older communities. The point is that data science is an exercise in unraveling the unknown for unseen correlations and causations. Teams competent in data science and teams that adopt and harness the power of data science (such as WalMart) will be the companies that thrive in the digital economy. Companies that insist on factory-hierarchy management will be the companies that perish in the digital economy.

Data science is uniquely weird, because it explores the unknown correlations, the statistical analysis, of what *might happen.* And going through the data discovery, applying a variety of algorithms, training a model, and then using the model in the real world, is a lot of uncertainty.

If we agree that every company in some form or fashion is a tech company, this identifies that data science/AI/ML, with all these uncertainties, are necessities to stay in business.

## 4.4.1 AI/ML Project Outline

- Concept capture: outcomes, audience, validation, prioritization, scope, and POR.
- Business team customer story capture, dashboard mockups.
- Business review: estimated cost and business value, ROI, or pricelist.
- Plan for delivery to production, observability, maintainability, support, enhancement
- Team digital infrastructure.
    - Way to post info: POR, validation, user stories, specs, API (wiki or similar)
    - Way to manage a task board and prioritize (AgileDevOps, IceScrum, wiki)
    - Way to do video calls and action items (MS Teams®, Slack®, GoogleMeet®)
    - Way to manage code/check-in/build/version/test (Github® or Azure® DevOps)
    - Way to message (Slack, MS Teams, or similar)
- Data Sandbox, security (one or more Docker images, enable logging, enable software/tool installs, accessible by team, inaccessible by others).
- Load data science tools into sandbox, load data into sandbox.
- *Data discovery >>> this is a biggie. It takes time and is not normally a part of IT projects.*
- Data wrangling (multiple data sources).
- Cohorts and hypothesis.
- Model/review, algorithm selection/optimization.
- Review first results.
- Data science refinement, defect cleanup, automated data cleanup.
- Establish dataflow/pub-sub for production.
- Model/review, algorithm selection/optimization.
- Observability reporting delivery.
- Transition to production, deliver containers, training, knowledge exchange.
- Use in production, capture feedback (add feedback form to app for ease and consistency).

The above are tools and processes to allow *people* to build and complete something together. It's not about the tools, it's not about the processes. It is about the people and the outcomes.

## 4.5 The Power of "Yet"

Failure is OK. This is such simple wisdom and it is applicable in the world of tech teams and our digital economy. Kindergarteners will say "I cannot tie my shoes." Kindergarten teachers will say, "That's OK, you cannot tie your shoes YET."

Thomas Edison, when a reporter asked him how it felt to fail 1,000 times in his attempts to invent the electric light, quipped: "I didn't fail 1,000 times. The light bulb was an invention of 1,000 steps."[2]

Taking risks is involved in any new endeavor. And with risk, failure sometimes happens. If failure never happens, you are most likely overindulging in risk avoidance, meaning your accomplishments are limited and your value is limited. Risk and failure are healthy, within reason. When you say "we haven't succeeded *yet*" you paint the picture that you will succeed sooner or later.

## 4.6 Trail Map and Conclusion

- Start with customer validation to identify the underserved market. Ask a wide spectrum of people the same question; sort the feedback to clarify who has what problems. Do business due diligence to confirm you are solving a high-value, time-sensitive problem.
- Innovation needs the right care and feeding. Focus on things that improve innovation (outcomes and success criteria), avoid things that hinder innovation (factory hierarchies, excessive involvement from functional management, micromanagement, matrix management, situations in which fear of being wrong drives decisions). These may work in other situations, but these do NOT work for innovation.
- Get started on data science. Capture agile user stories, mock up dashboards. Start on a Proof of concept project to simply prove there is business value in data science.

---

[2] https://quotefancy.com/quote/916587/Thomas-A-Edison-I-didn-t-fail-1000-times
-The-light-bulb-was-an-invention-with-1000-steps

# Chapter 5

# Remote Teams Capability Model

## 5.1 Factory-Era Management By Control Fails in Digital Era

Factory-era management by control is very different from digital economy management by outcomes or power metrics. In the control-heavy tech companies I have worked at, execution is high friction, continuous improvement is forgotten, and innovation is non-existent. In these control situations, employees are evaluated on factory measures that are irrelevant in digital economy: Did they arrive on-time? Leave early? Do what they were told? Emphasis: measuring individuals rather than measuring team outcomes. When individuals (rather than groups) are evaluated, innovation suffers. Put yourself in the shoes of an individual contributor:

*"I should just do as my boss says without taking initiative and definitely avoid making my peers appear more competent than I am."*

In these situations, the failing is not due to the employees. The failing is due to executives who watch and reward behavior that is low value and inconsequential. At the end of the quarter, the balance sheet isn't changed by good or bad attendance or even lines of code—it is changed by solving high-value, time-sensitive problems for your customers differently and better than the alternatives from the competition.

In summary, value creation matters, attendance is inconsequential. Teams create value. There is a *giant* gap between management focused on control (such as measuring good attendance) and management focused on value creation (such as solving big problems for your customers which are different and better than alternatives) measured by key success criteria.

Measuring individuals showing up to work on time is truly meaningless, counterproductive, and well documented in many failed ranking-and-rating evaluations systems.

The remedy is obvious—enable your teams to solve big problems, give them whitespace not micromanagement, give them clear goals (don't make them guess), and trust them to execute. Measure the key success criteria as a team. Tell the team the key success criteria at the beginning of the project, don't make them guess, and don't change success criteria on a whim.

Measuring team success is the keystone of encouraging collaboration. Measuring team success is the means to encourage one team member to help another. This brings us to observation of our primitive wiring in the modern digital era (see Figure 5.1).

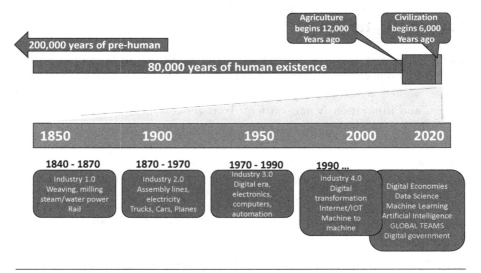

**Figure 5.1**   Our Evolution and the Modern Workplace

Why does this matter? The short answer: Factory controls are fine for factories; factory controls simply fail in digital era workplaces.

The longer answer: We have been wired by 80,000 years (around 4,000 generations) of existence. Then the modern workplace landed on us 200 years ago (only 10 generations). (Yes, I acknowledge there are many exceptions, but just go with me for a minute). Management by command and control is simply an extension of pack or tribe hierarchy.

The digital era and the knowledge worker are two human generations old. Yes, there are exceptions to this, but the logic still applies; our primitive wiring involving pack or tribe hierarchy hasn't caught up. Our primitive wiring is still an impediment to our growth as a society.

*There are ways to overcome these primitive impediments to our teams, our careers, and ourselves.* In fact, there are many good examples of how to overcome these workplace challenges, and these directly pertain to effective remote tech teams.

The first step recognizes that management by command and control is a dreadfully wrong approach for Industry 4.0 and for knowledge workers. When Execs spend the majority of their time and energy on the internal workings of the company, they are left with very little time to  understand (even partially) the complex, rapidly changing, shades-of-grey world in which knowledge workers live and breathe every working hour. One would conclude that managers and executives understand this and consciously avoid top-down, one-way discussions. And while there are many examples of healthy organizations (e.g., Microsoft®) that have evolved past command and control and are making a conscious effort to measure outcomes, not outputs, regrettably, most organizations are ego driven and coin operated—"I pay you to do X, so do X" attracts the wrong type of managers and repels the right type of workers. We will get to the remedies, but first we need to fully understand the problem of our work, of our workplaces, and of our wiring.

This directly applies to the maturity model covered in this chapter.

## 5.2 Top-Down Orgs and Top-Down Processes

### 5.2.1 Top Down Fails Tech

It's possible for factory managers to have an understanding of factory inputs and outputs, and it's possible for factory managers to learn/know how to build cheaper and still build high quality.

However, the top-down approach fails tech. It's simply not possible for someone at the top of an organizational hierarchy to have the knowledge to do technical micromanagement.

Regrettably, tribal hierarchies are part of our deepest instincts. It is possible for someone at the top of a big organization to set outcomes and then let self-managing teams execute. But that requires consciously rejecting the tribal hierarchy.

Top-down organizations mirror top-down factory processes: the executives direct, the subordinates do the work. That's workable as long as the executives give the right directions. In digital economies, applying top-down, factory-style management has been known to fail frequently. Here are some highlights of epic top-down failures:

- Top-down management failed the Soviet Union. Their socialist system (sort of) worked in the first industrial era, 1910–1950, when all they needed was agriculture and rail. The soviet socialist economy (sort of) survived in the second industrial era of electronics from 1950–1980. And the Soviet Union imploded in the early '80s.
- Top-down management failed the airline industry. A large airline headquartered in Dallas, a large airline headquartered in New York City, and a smaller airline headquartered in Atlantic City all went bankrupt in the late '90s, at a time when data warehousing and data science were available and being used to great effect by WalMart. The (avoidable) root cause of all three failures relate to top-down management who neglected to invest, or seriously embrace, the technical infrastructure to capture and analyze customer demand, feedback, and sentiment.
- Top-down management failed the tech industry. In the 1980s and 1990s, a New York company owned the market of mini-computers selling for less than $100,000. At their peak they employed 140,000 people. Within a decade of their peak business, they were  acquired, and soon after that their products were discontinued. Top-down factory management led them to focus internally rather than externally on the market and customers. Had they listened, they could have adjusted the business model to effectively sell personal computers, but did not. Another tech innovator and manufacturer of SPARC-based servers and workstations had the best products on the market and were soon after acquired for a paltry $7B. Again, the root causes were internal focus typical of factory-style management, a lack of external market focus, and lack of informed, data-driven decision making.
- Top-down management failed retail. Remember the two Chicago-based retail giants who merged? They had data warehousing, they had data, just like their main competitor, WalMart. But the Chicago retailers failed to gainfully use that data. The merger resulted in bankruptcy, while WalMart emerged as the largest business in the world; the reason relates to operations which embrace the digital economy and rejected factory-style top-down management.

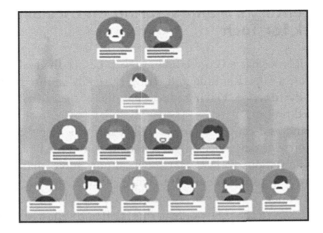

**Figure 5.2**   Last Century's Top-Down Process for Factories

These were *all* viable businesses. They had competitive product. They had critical mass. All they had to do was not shoot themselves in the foot. But they did. Top-down management fails for complex-task knowledge workers.

## 5.2.2 Our Outdated Management Wiring

- Factory boss says "do this" to subordinate line boss
- Line boss says "do this" to subordinate warehouse boss
- Warehouse boss says "do this" to subordinate worker

This approach was a reasonable tool for straightforward manufacturing types of tasks.

No surprise, this closely mirrors social hierarchies (see Figure 5.2).

Ego-driven "big boss" types had the drive and did what was necessary to get to the top and stay there. Bear in mind, getting to the top is typically not based on merit.

Once they arrived at the top, they treated subordinates as they were treated: not bothering to listen or respond to complaints; indulging in continuous improvement but only if it was their idea; typically, low on data, measuring attendance and factory line production.

The 20th century sees management science improve and evolve. Manufacturing metrics are logged. And, sure, if you measure it, it will be done—if you measure attendance, people show up on time (mostly). If you measure output, people assemble more pumps, or bail more hay (mostly).

## 5.3 Last Century's Manufacturing Metrics Simply Don't Work for Tech

Individual attendance has no correlation to outcomes. Individual output is irrelevant if the project fails. Ranking and rating is usually counterproductive and usually creates dysfunction. Having functional silos of specialists creates lag and frequently failed projects.

This command-and-control approach fails badly when applied for information workers, software developers, digital marketers, and the like, for the simple reason that information workers, developers, know more than their supervisors. They know how to attain outcomes, while the managers are measuring the wrong stuff: attendance or defects or lines of code. While it is very possible for supervisors to listen to the info workers, this is often disallowed by our ancient wiring—our egos drive us to a higher place in the pack, disallows us to really listen. And with many levels of management shouting from the top, it is impossible for the people in the middle to hear the people on the front line if those front-line people know more than those up the management chain.

Organizations faced the challenge: change or die.

The factory career ladder is, unfortunately, alive and well.

- Factory career ladder means you started as a line worker doing repetitive tasks.
- You did what your boss said, and worked your way up to more complex tasks.
- Next, you did what your boss said and demonstrated skill in managing a line.
- Next you did what your boss said and worked several lines.
- Next you did what your boss said and worked in an office.

On this ladder, your value and your boss's value is knowledge of how this particular operation operates. The common theme is that your boss tells you what to do. Typically, the boss talks, you listen, in a one-directional conversation (we've all been there).

Shifting the conversation away from C&C process (admittedly, it's like the car wreck you cannot look away from, but still exhausting), we can objectively compare manufacturing processes to software and scientific processes.

*In manufacturing, there is a process:*

- Specify the end product, including bill of materials and assembly instructions
- Stage the raw materials
- Assemble
- Implement quality assurance
- Measure and improve efficiency and defects

The manufacturing process involves very little discovery, experimentation, or the like.

Manufacturing organizations are typically top-down management hierarchies, and manufacturing processes and top down management hierarchies are fine for manufacturing but badly fail tech and knowledge workers. Let's unpack some different processes.

*In construction there is an engineering process:*

- Concept formation of the building, campus, roadway, or factory
- Plan: Blueprint and specify instructions to construction teams
- Review
- Bid, award
- Build: Construction teams pour the concrete, drive the nails
- Inspect and approve
- Occupy

*In science, there is a scientific process:*

- Observe
- Question
- Hypothesis
- Experiment, controlled testing
- Gather data, refine or reject hypothesis
- Reach conclusions

*Agile software:*

- User stories, prioritization, thoughtful work breakdown (sprint goal)
- Focus and execute, scrum focus, small batch size, frequent handoffs, constant pace
- Reduce multitasking, reduce large batch
- Establish sprint, establish definition of success, define key results/outcomes
- Modularize, define ins and outs
- Collaborate, build and self-test
- Readiness, trials
- Deploy, measurable key results/outcomes

Software is most like the scientific process. Software includes a discovery-and-design process that is absent in construction or manufacturing.

Let us be clear: top down can work fine for many situations, but top down simply does not work for tech, knowledge workers, and the digital economy. Top-down management is a hard habit to break because of our tribal wiring, our tribal hierarchy wiring, and our primitive egos.

*Stop using top-down management for tech, knowledge work, and digital economies.* Instead manage by outcome and by power metrics such as customer satisfaction, and focus on team performance and less on individual performance.

### 5.3.1 A Cautionary Tale of Innovation in a Top-Down Manufacturing Tech Company

This tech company has a desire to innovate. This company manufactures hardware and has a manufacturing hierarchy and manufacturing process mindset. The company directed employees to "go innovate." Our team carried out the directive and, to the best of our abilities, tackled the innovation problems. The innovation task produced multiple concepts, each with reasonable detail.

Executives didn't want to hear about customers or markets; they just wanted to hear about the technology. At executive review we hear, "How long is this going to take?" "What revenues will it generate?"

In the regrettable final act of this PowerPoint® drama, executives, based on gut feel and nothing more, pursued a low-value, high-risk project to make a cheaper product, discarding high-value projects that they couldn't be bothered to understand—they just didn't "get it." My observation: this was factory hierarchy top-down management in action. This situation was more about the execs, with primitive tribal brain wiring and egos. Facts, market validation, and scientific process were missing in action.

The next day, we were told to do more "innovation" and prepare innovation strategy version 2. Clearly, they were not serious, they were just going through the motions—and our role was valueless. I found other employment, and many co-workers did too. The folks still employed there are just going through the motions, lacking the capability, resources, and motivation to innovate. No surprise, job satisfaction is low and attrition is high.

The alternative (advisable) approach could have been:

- **Properly resource:** Allocate some reasonable R&D budget.
- **Develop concepts:** Face market—what problems are we solving, what is the desired outcome?
- **Validate with customers and partners:** Is this a real problem, is it high value and without workaround?
- **Plan for sales:** Is there a viable path to market? Can we sell it efficiently? Do we need to adjust the sales force? Do we need to adjust awareness and demand creation?
- **Prioritize:** Based on available data (validation, tech assessment, sales feedback) do a weighted scoring and prioritize.
- **Apply scientific process:** Prototype, create proof of concept for the top of the priority list.

Hardware organizations have these simple choices:

1. Be a factory, leave the innovation to others.
2. Innovate without proper resources or funding and expect consistent failure.

3. Innovate with proper resources and funding and plan to bring to market at least some of the products of the innovation effort.

Nothing wrong with option 1. Don't expect significant growth. Option 2 burns limited funds and talent without any return. Don't expect significant growth. Option 3 is the only real method to survive and thrive in a digital economy. Teams innovate.

## 5.4 Maturity Model—Effective Remote Teams

Effective remote projects are necessary for organizations to compete in the coming decades and in the digital economy, and our destination of effective remote organizations able to compete in the coming decade is not instant—it takes effort and change. Building an effective organization takes care and feeding of others, and when done right, everyone wins.

Starting with the end in mind, the Effective Remote Tech Teams Maturity Model is a roadmap to an improved organization, better equipped to compete and thrive in the era of digital economies.

All companies are less than perfect, but some are better than others, and some are more mature in their journey. I believe today's Microsoft is a great, real-world example of an *effective* remote organization.

Satya Nadella, in *Hit Refresh*,[1] states:

*Microsoft has always been at its best when it connects personal passion to a broader purpose: Windows, Office, Xbox, Surface, our servers, and the Microsoft Cloud.*

In this statement, Mr. Nadella appeals to our instincts to belong and become.

To clearly understand where you are and objectively identify improvements, we will unpack this maturity model step by step. See Figure 5.3.

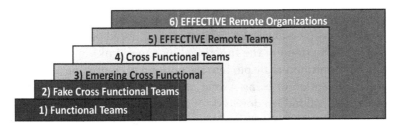

**Figure 5.3** Capabilities Maturity Model for Remote Tech Teams

---

[1] https://news.microsoft.com/hitrefresh/

### 5.4.1 Functional Teams: Maturity Level 1 (You Gotta Start Somewhere)

This level puts the tech team (or content creator, or website manager) into generating the code or content without really understanding the objective. The contributors are in an uncomfortable position of guessing, leaning on the functional supervisors for all the minutiae. Then the functional manager's response can be immediate and complete, or late and less than complete. (See Figure 5.4.)

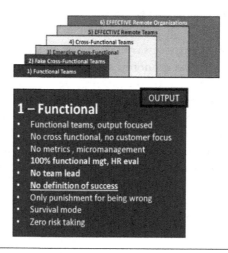

**Figure 5.4**   Maturity Level 1

This frequently leads to a non-meritocracy, because projects without a definition of success are also without meaningful metrics. Managers (consciously or subconsciously) play favorites and assign choice assignments to friends (often involving workplace bias) and therefore the crappy assignments go to others lower on the friend list (again, often involving workplace bias). Crappy assignments result in crappy evaluations, limited raises, limited promotions—all based on the subjective opinion of the functional manager (yuk).

In addition, contributors are put into the position of competing with teammates to avoid the perception of being wrong or inadequate. This stifles collaboration and growth. The real hidden downside of an *output* focus rather than an *outcome* focus is the resulting lack of motivation, lack of initiative, and lack of enthusiasm.

With fair winds, when things are good, the negatives are diminished and tolerable, and typically execs and HR only hear the good news. Even in the good times, these environments are mostly stick and no carrot, meaning mostly punishment/criticism for things perceived to be wrong and no counterbalancing reward for things accomplished and well done. The safe choice is to wait for specific directions, follow those directions to the letter, and don't worry about anything (or anyone) else. In these environments, why would any contributor take a risk or even take personal initiative?

But when things go poorly, the horns come out and white-knuckled behavior magnifies. The work environment becomes increasingly intolerable. This leads to a toxic environment in which the complainers win and the producers don't. This often leads to everyone looking out only for themselves, not the team. Collaboration diminishes. Teams become increasingly less effective. Projects fail. Customer satisfaction suffers. Earnings suffer. Talent leaves. Headcount gets cut.

To be fair, it is not *always* this way, but more often than not it is—I've witnessed it firsthand. There are good pockets in the worst of companies. I've been a part of functional teams in which I had benevolent and fair managers. But even then, those benevolent managers faced headwinds by their peers, and toxicity influenced business outcomes (especially customer satisfaction and competitiveness).

There is a silver lining, a positive example: today's Microsoft.

Microsoft has not always been a great place to work. Microsoft in the middle years (output) was demonstrably awful. Now, compare to today's Microsoft: Nadella's focus on outcomes has resulted in a significantly above average place to work, and Microsoft's bottom line over recent years speaks for itself.

The reason I bring this up is that poorly run companies can change, as Microsoft has, and financial rewards have come from this change (Microsoft's financial results bear witness).

*How this is relevant for this book:* The hallmark of Level 1 is the absence of a clear definition of success, which puts everyone into survival mode. And survival instincts shout down other parts of our brain, which motivate us with our more positive instincts to belong and become.

Next step on the journey—please understand *and avoid* Maturity Level (2), Fake Cross-Functional Teams and Maturity Level (3), Emerging Cross-Functional Teams, and go directly to Maturity Level (4), Cross Functional Teams—meaning empowered team leads, with focus on outputs and remote contributors with the same status as headquarters-based contributors.

## 5.4.2 Fake Cross-Functional Teams: Maturity Level 2

Fake cross-functional teams happen when some sales/marketing/QA/UI or similar folks are thrown together, often with a team lead but without a clear definition of success and without an empowered leader (see Figure 5.5).

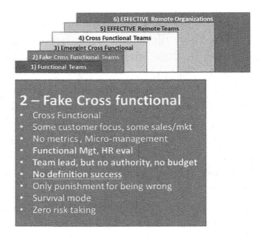

**Figure 5.5**   Fake Cross-Functional Teams

The missing ingredients are lack of shared definition of success (aka, no clarity on outcomes). The team lead is without authority or budget: missing team success evaluation, still using individual output evaluation.

Not helping matters is ongoing involvement and distraction by functional management and HR.

Basically, fake cross-functional teams are just going through the motions, without real change. Functional managers will micromanage and frequently will disrupt the project by re-assigning or re-prioritizing contributor work.

*How this is relevant for this book*: For remote teams, Level 2, the fake cross-functional team approach, continues to suffer from output rather than outcome thinking, typically lacking any shared goals or definition of success, meaning contributors are still guessing and fearful of being wrong. This leads to survival mode, and survival instincts shout down other parts of our brain which drive our more positive instincts to belong and become.

It's worth repeating the next step on the journey: please understand *and avoid* Maturity Level (2) Fake Cross-Functional Teams and Maturity Level (3), Emerging Cross-Functional Teams, and go directly to Maturity Level (4), Cross-Functional Teams—meaning empowered team leads with focus on outputs and remote contributors with the same status as headquarters-based contributors.

### 5.4.3 Emerging Cross-Functional Teams: Maturity Level 3

Emerging cross-functional teams happen when some of the pieces are in place. When tech, QA, Tech Pubs, training, UI, and content people work alongside

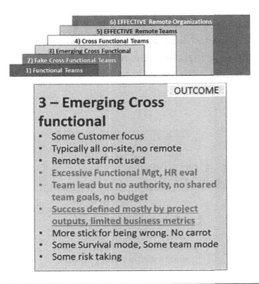

**Figure 5.6**   Emerging Cross-Functional Teams

customer-facing sales, services, marketing, partner managers, actual partners, and similar folks—with clear definition of success (see Figure 5.6).

The big hurdle remains shifting from output to outcome, meaning an empowered program manager or team lead has authority, and ongoing involvement by functional management and HR happens but is 100% supportive of project outcomes, and 0% distracting from project outcomes. This is hard, because it's hard to keep focused on the important when the urgent keeps interrupting.

*This is highly relevant for this book:* For remote teams, when the team has a clear picture of success, when the team has shared goals, focusing on outcomes not outputs, this leads to remote contributors having the same status as headquarters-based contributors. This leads to contributors knowing what's needed—they no longer need to guess, they stop being fearful of being wrong. Collaboration is valued, and this dissipates survival mode and magnifies our more positive instincts to belong and become.

The next step on the journey to *effective* remote teams and *effective* remote organizations are truly exciting, rewarding, and gratifying.

## 5.4.4 Cross-Functional Teams: Maturity Level 4

Real cross-functional teams happen when tech, QA, Tech Pubs, training, UI, and content people work alongside customer-facing sales, services, marketing, partner managers, actual partners, and similar folks—with a clear definition of success, with an empowered leader. The big hurdle remains shifting from outputs to outcomes and shifting the authority to an empowered program manager or team lead. This means reduced ongoing involvement by functional management and HR (see Figure 5.7).

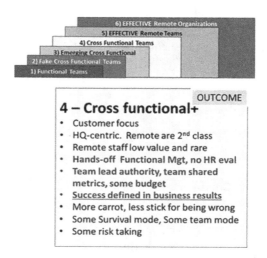

**Figure 5.7**   Cross-Functional Teams

Not every activity is a cross-functional team activity, and some staff can be assigned to take care of the day-to-day urgent tasks. This may require some staff/org changes, and it may require some functional managers and HR to take on significantly diminished roles. These folks have the option of transitioning into an empowered team lead role or finding some other role involving functional micromanagement.

A real-world example of this can be observed in the role of a Microsoft program manager. This is not wishful thinking; it works for Microsoft (and others).

*This is highly relevant for this book:* For remote teams, when the team has a clear picture of success, when the team has shared goals, focusing on outcomes not outputs, this leads to remote contributors having the same status as headquarters-based contributors. This leads to contributors know what's needed—they no longer need to guess, they stop being fearful of being wrong. Collaboration is valued, and this dissipates survival mode and magnifies our more positive instincts to belong and become.

The next step on the journey to *effective* remote teams and *effective* remote organizations are truly exciting and rewarding.

### 5.4.5 Effective Remote Teams: Maturity Level 5

Effective remote tech teams happen when tech, QA, Tech Pubs, training, UI, and content people work alongside customer-facing sales, services, marketing, partner managers, actual partners, and similar folks, with a clear definition of success, with an empowered leader. (See Figure 5.8.) Here we have fully shifted from outputs to outcomes. The authority (and accountability) is fully shifted to empowered program managers or team leads.

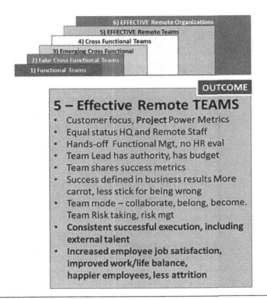

**Figure 5.8**  Effective Remote Teams

The effective remote tech team maturity shows itself when projects are consistently successful, as measured by project power metrics. And these projects include remote contributors as equal participants regardless of whether they are local or remote, full-time, or contracted employees.

*This is highly relevant for this book:* For remote teams, when the team has a clear picture of success, when the team has shared goals, focusing on outcomes not outputs, this leads to remote contributors having the same status as headquarters-based contributors. This leads to contributors know what's needed—they no longer need to guess, they stop being fearful of being wrong. Collaboration is valued, and this dissipates survival mode and magnifies our more positive instincts to belong and become.

The next step on the journey to *effective* remote teams and *effective* remote organizations are truly exciting and rewarding.

### 5.4.6 Effective Remote Organizations: Maturity Level 6

When organization-level outcomes and power metrics are understood, then middle managers don't have to guess, they *know* what to focus on. Knowing what success looks like as defined by business results (not by micromanagement) is truly energizing. This requires change, and the reward makes the effort worthwhile (see Figure 5.9).

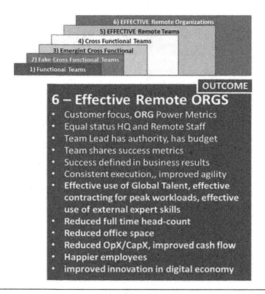

**Figure 5.9**   Effective Remote Organizations

Changes include being consistent with outcomes and power metrics from executives, to HR, to functional management. If teams are tasked and empowered to achieve specific results, it is highly counterproductive for functional management to indulge in micromanagement. Tasking and empowering a team means execs and functional managers and HR must accept the team results even when the team takes a different path to accomplish the results.

When organizations become skilled at effective remote teams, the organization benefits are many:

- Greater employee satisfaction
- Improved organizational skills and capabilities
- Competitive advantage
- No need for micromanagement with self-managed teams, making remote work more practical

Add to that,

- Reduction in permanent office expenses
- The ability to bring on specialized temporary talent
- The ability to be frugal on OpX during business cycles when headcount is not required

 When remote, am I visible? Do I have a place and a purpose? Self-managed tech teams, working on shared outcomes, replace doubts, which excite survival response with sense of place and purpose, which excites happier brain chemistry, leading to both positive motivation and innovation.

**BEST METHODS**

» Measure the right stuff: outcomes. Stop focusing on individual performance and functional management, rather focus on team outcomes, not individual behaviors (this includes functional managers and HR).

» Yes, change is hard. It requires serious changes to functional management and HR. It runs contrary to our tribal hierarchy wiring.

# Chapter 6

# Improvements for the Whole Organization

Every company is now a tech company. At a minimum, customer engagement, awareness, and demand all depend on web presence. Most companies employ basic e-commerce, digital payment, ad insertion, Google® marketing, and digital content.

- Technology is an ingredient. Technology is a tool, not an outcome.
- Technology alone does not result in business relevant outcomes.
- But technology with continuous improvement is mandatory in a digital economy.

Real organizational improvements require focusing on *outcomes*. Satya Nadella, CEO of Microsoft®, refers to these as *power metrics*. These are in addition to normal quarterly earnings and the like. Power metrics focus on *outcomes*, not *outputs*—outcomes directly related to customer values:

- Wider customer adoption
- Improved customer satisfaction
- Improved partner performance
- Improved partner satisfaction

Power metrics are achieved through projects with goals and key success criteria aligned to these power metrics and customer values. In order to deliver improvements—customer values—cross-functional teams (including sales and marketing) will interlock with technical contributors to clarify needed customer values in a way that can be acted upon by the tech contributors.

In concept, cross-functional teams are easy.

- In reality, cross-functional teams fail when evaluations are based on inconsequential or individual measures.
- In reality, cross-functional teams fail when functional managers are at cross-purposes with project leaders or when functional managers micromanage.
- In reality, cross-functional teams fail when functional managers expect staff "stretch."
- External resources are disallowed by functional managers due to lack of control.

To achieve the desired power metrics evaluations, we need to change to measure team outcomes, and functional managers will deal with day-to-day emergencies without disrupting resources allocated to project work.

To achieve the desired power metrics, companies will be capable of properly staffing peaks and valleys using external resources effectively rather than attempting to make staff stretch.

## 6.1 Trust, the Bigger Picture

Trust starts with teams but impacts the entire business. In our search to improve leader-to-contributor team relationships and bigger-picture business-to-employee relationships, we can learn from business transactions and business relationships.

From *Rules to Break and Laws to Follow*[1], Peppers and Rogers offer basics of customer retention. These lessons are equally applicable to contributor motivation and contributor retention.

1. Customers will do business with you tomorrow only if they (and their friends) trust you today. Therefore, *customer trust is a prerequisite for long-term business success*. In a sense, your employees are also your customers. They spend the finite hours in their careers working on your goals at your direction. Just like your customers have a choice, your employees also have a choice.
2. Your employees will work to earn customer trust only if they trust you, their employer. So your job is to (a) *motivate your employees to treat customers*

---

[1] Peppers, D., and Rogers, M. (2008) *Rules to Break and Laws to Follow: How Your Business Can Beat the Crisis of Short-Termism.* ISBN: 978-0-470-22754-1. Wiley.

*fairly,* and (b) *enable them to do so by providing the right tools, training, and authority for taking action.*

These two-party business transactions also apply to teams and team trust. Trust matters for contributors, just like trust matters for customers. A contributor can choose to spend the limited years, months, and days of their careers with you, or they can spend them elsewhere. Building team trust, just like building customer trust, is the keystone of a long-term, mutually beneficial relationship.

Building trust with contributors starts by measuring *team* outcomes, rather than *individual* outputs. The days of measuring output (like a factory) are long gone. Measuring output like lines of code, bugs fixed, ranking+rating in a digital economy doesn't result in business results. Measuring cross-functional team outcomes generates business results in the digital economy.

Measuring individual output frequently creates distrust and is frequently counterproductive. Measuring individual productivity is OK when things are going well, *but,* when things go poorly, measuring individual output *is toxic*—our survival instincts kick in, we stop thinking logically, we form snap judgments without really listening, we stop collaborating, we stop taking risk for fear of being wrong, our genuine empathy disappears. When things go poorly, measuring individual output can lead to taking credit for someone else's work or placing unwarranted blame or criticism. In digital economy settings in which teams are constantly attempting to innovate and setbacks are commonplace, this is unacceptable. Why would anyone want to work at a place like that?

*Team trust can be created with shared goals*—a focus on solving shared problems in cross-functional teams to achieve a shared outcome (aka, Microsoft® power metrics) such as customer feedback, customer sentiment, increased customer usage. These approaches are proven to work at Microsoft and are equally applicable in smaller settings.

- Outcome focus: Team shares the same goals.
- Outcome focus: Encourages people to solve problems in their own way.
- Outcome focus: Diminishes or eliminates the importance of individual evaluations.
- Outcome focus: Measures a short and simple list of the right outcomes.
- Outcome focus: Makes those outcomes known at the beginning of the project.
- Outcome focus: Avoids changing the goals.

*Outcomes* matter, *outputs* don't. Focusing on shared team outcomes builds success and builds trust. Now, more than ever, trust is essential in remote teams.

### 6.1.1 Creating Trust Starts with Engaging and Consistency

#### Real Life Story

Decades ago, I worked for NCR®, and the company had problems, so many problems. Changes were made, a new CEO, Lars Nyberg, was hired. Lars was awesome; he directly addressed *all* 15,000 NCR employees every month. He did a brief (10–20 minute) video, VHS copies of which were distributed worldwide. He wanted the video to be seen by everyone. The monthly "Lars Video" was viewed at all team meetings, with managers present.

The format was consistent: (1) some good news, (2) some "needs work," and (3) some general management guidance. The call to action was consistent: discuss with your team, discuss with your manager. This formed the means of closed-loop feedback to front-line management up to executive management, if warranted.

His guidance included this memorable quote: "Push decisions into the hands of the people closest to the problem—they are most qualified." This was 20+ years ago and was a refreshing change from top-down hierarchical management. Seeing Lars speak, seeing his body language, and hearing his deliberate language imparted both trust and credibility. Lars did not try to be someone he wasn't. He was not high energy or charismatic, nor did he attempt to exert any force of personality. He was himself, very genuine and highly credible. The kind of leader who everyone wanted to be with. Using his VHS tapes, Lars effectively implemented a frequent and high-value "all hands" to a very large worldwide company with tens of thousands of employees.

Fast forward to present day, we now all have video conferencing. So, a "Lars-style all hands" monthly video call is not just possible, it's easy and near zero cost. As we are remote, executive presence is more valuable, more impactful, and more mandatory than ever.

Do a monthly Lars-style all hands. Why not? It serves to connect the remote personnel to organizational leadership and impart a shared sense of place: you belong to the bigger group with a shared sense of purpose—the shared goals of the organization.

Remote (and video conferencing) presents an incredible opportunity for executives to be *more* present and engaged. Executives can offer to informally join the occasional team meeting. This can be just five minutes to communicate the team's importance in the bigger picture, reiterate the goals and key results, and say thanks for the hard work (catch them doing something right).

---

**BEST METHODS**

Executive video conference for monthly all hands. And executive appearances at team meetings show the team is not invisible. The team does matter. The team does have a place and a purpose.

When remote, am I visible? Do I matter? Do I have a place and a purpose?

## 6.2 Power Metrics Contrasted with Functional Control

Old-school management focusing on control, functions, and individuals was acceptable in the factories of the last century. But "control" management is an epic failure in our digital age.

Now, in the digital age, outcome-focused management wins. Cross-functional groups with shared goals can produce highly desirable and measurable outcomes. Customer satisfaction, customer retention, increased business per customer are "power metrics."

Satya Nadella (CEO Microsoft) had these statements on power metrics[2]: [paraphrased and re-ordered]

- Our discipline on how we think about metrics: we measure *performance metrics* such as quarterly earnings, profit, and the like. We also measure *power metrics* such as customer satisfaction, usage metrics, things that will make a difference longer term.
- Why do we even exist? We talk about our mission to empower every person and every organization to achieve more. Why does anyone want to work at Microsoft?
- Customers don't care about your organization. But your organization is important, as it is a way to be relevant to your customers. We bring multiple teams together in seeking what customers care about. We talk about customer use cases and solutions.

Nadella paints a clear picture of improving customer satisfaction by using teams with common/shared goals. Microsoft's stock price and valuation is a statement on the success of this approach.

The concept of power metrics is clear and measurable for cross-functional teams. But power metrics are less workable for individuals or functional departments.

Here's a real-world example of cross-functional teams missing in action. While I was at NCR, our software team developed best-in-class server failover for both Unix® and NT. Regrettably, marketing failed to execute. Our failover software was mentioned once—a single line item on a single brochure. In this

---

[2]  https://www.linkedin.com/posts/anabotin_we-had-the-pleasure-to-have-satya-nadella-ugcPost-6688760498613194752-qf1D

case marketing was missing in action. We spent 10 people for a year but couldn't be bothered to tell anyone about it. The root cause of the disconnect was not an unwilling marketing manager—he was fine. The root cause was the conflicting direction given by his supervision (marketing group functional managers). If these functional managers in marketing had been properly tasked with power metrics—adoption, satisfaction, etc.—it is safe to say business results would have been improved.

Change is hard. In order for power metrics to succeed, functional management must take a role secondary to team leads.

As you transition from functional-led to team-led organization, you will encounter headwinds. There are those who believe that strong functional management will just do the right thing. There are those who believe that strong functional management with weak team leads are okay. In principle this is believable, in reality conflicting demands will occur, and the organization will revert back to unproductive behaviors.

Functional managers will usually grudgingly cooperate with cross-functional teams. And functional managers have been known to prioritize the urgent ahead of the important and siphon off resources to do random tasks without bothering to consider or even communicate with impacted teams. This is where functional management can and should better align to power metrics concepts.

## 6.2.1 Outcomes over Output

### Hypothetical Project—ARM-Based Server CPU Computer Chip

Great in concept, recognizing other server CPUs over the years have become overdesigned, gotten too expensive, and consume too much power, this startup builds a server chip with significantly lower price and lower power with good enough performance. (See Table 6.1.)

The only problem is, the message to customers and investors is wishful thinking. There is no proof and no path to attain proof—just guys with slides. Only this wasn't hypothetical . . . this was a real Austin startup, $100M in funding, and it was an *epic* failure.

This real team working on a real project delivered on the shortest possible schedule. It was a little cheaper, it was lower power, and in the interest of schedule, the team did not include multi-threading. Accordingly, performance did look good on paper, but without multi-threading it failed real benchmarks. The investments in rounds A, B, C raised $100M. After first silicon, benchmarking, and customer rejection, investors refused a round D.

*Output focus, NOT best practices.* The original plan focused on output (deliver the chip), not outcome (win in the market). The tech team had low confidence of

## Table 6.1  The Cautionary Tale of Output vs. Outcome

| | |
|---|---|
| (Output, *ineffective*)<br><br>The message to customers and investors—our ARM-based server CPU computer chip: | Will double industry benchmarks.<br>Will cost half the price of competition.<br>Will consume half the power of the competition.<br>Will have same or better performance.<br>Will meet Dell server schedules (target delivery = x date).<br>In two years, will have 17% of server CPU market. |
| (Output, *ineffective*)<br><br>The message to the tech team—our goal is: build an ARM-based server CPU computer chip: | On the shortest possible schedule, to hit Dell server schedules (target delivery = x date).<br>It needs to be cheaper than competition.<br>It needs to be lower power than competition.<br>It needs to have similar performance as competition. |
| **(Outcome! Effective!)**<br><br>Our goal is: build an ARM-based Server CPU computer chip.<br><br>Key success criteria: | Compare to x86 model xyz.<br>Match or better performance measured by FIO benchmark for core equivalent.<br>Cheaper measured by $/core equivalent.<br>25% lower power consumption as measured by watts/core equivalent.<br>Schedule is a secondary concern, ideally meet Dell server schedules (target delivery = x date) |

success, the business team thought it would be wildly successful. All the vague stuff created a bad workplace, and the tech team was unable to work smoothly with the business team.

*Outcome focus, best practices.* Observe the simple changes and focus on outcome.

We replace "similar performance" (no yardstick), with "performance measured by FIO," a specific benchmark needed for industry adoption (FIO exercises multi-threading).

We replace "cheaper" (no yardstick) with "cheaper measured by $/core equivalent," avoiding an unfair chip-to-chip comparison and using a more objective core-to-core comparison.

We replace "lower power" (no yardstick) with "cheaper measured by watts/core equivalent," avoiding an unfair chip-to-chip comparison and using a more objective core-to-core comparison, where a lower performance core with much lower cost and power can compete with higher-performance core with much higher cost and higher power.

We replaced "shortest possible schedule dictated by external customer" with "schedule as secondary concern." We optimized efforts to build the right product, not the fastest time to market with the wrong product. The company can survive missing a Dell design in (Dell is not the only customer on the planet). The company cannot survive the failed design. And in this real-world example, the company did not survive.

An important concession on outcome focus: ideally our output is win 25% revenue share in the cloud data center server CPU market. This leaves product success criteria as unknown and is too vague for a product team to efficiently execute on. The alternative outcome focus is on customer choice and be the preferred customer choice based on known customer key purchase criteria—power, price, performance. With an existing comparative product (e.g., the x86 model xyz), this is possible.

◊ In the original plan: schedule first, get it to run, worry about the other vague stuff later (this actually happened in real life, causing a startup with a staff of 200+ to abruptly shut down).

◊ The improved plan: price, performance, and power are all known and measurable. We will have problems designing for the FIO benchmark; let's get the right performance help to design for success.

**BEST PRACTICES**

In the improved plan: Outcome based (win the market) with specific measurable key success criteria makes it possible to design for success and find the right uses for this innovative product.

## 6.3 The Myth of Regional Talent Hubs

This brings us to the question of how to find talent, how to afford talent, and how to put talent to the best possible use across entire organizations.

Great universities do create regional economic success, which builds better universities. But, increasingly, university education credentials are no longer the sole indicator of tech talent. We all know highly talented co-workers who are the product of less prestigious educations (even those who self-educated).

- Steve Jobs, a massive success at Apple. Did not graduate.
- John Sculley, *not* a success at Apple. Is a UPenn Wharton graduate.
- Tim Cook, a massive success at Apple. Is an Auburn University graduate, me too!

And, we all know co-workers with below-average talent who are the product of Ivy League schools. I am not bashing Ivy League schools, I have personally worked with brilliant Stanford grads (shoutout to Amber Huffman); I have also worked with duds who are Stanford grads. Not all graduates are superstars—far from it.

Increasingly, everyone will code in some form or fashion. Once upon a time, not everyone could use email, a word processor, a spreadsheet, or presentation software. Prior to that era, not everyone could type—we had typing pools.

*In the next decade, we will all be coders, we will be capable of basic coding, basic data science, machine learning, and statistics. Increasingly, we see easy-to-use programming languages and low-code programming tools. These are rapidly evolving to low-code data science, machine learning, and statistics.*

And, thankfully, the Internet, YouTube, and online courses deliver education worldwide to everyone with an Internet connection and a device. Anyone with a bit of ambition and a good work ethic can self-educate and remotely participate in the global digital economy.

### 6.3.1 Global Talent Pools

#### Talent—The Competitive Advantage or the Competitive Disadvantage

Consider the benefits to your organization if you could recruit from a talent pool beyond commuting distance to your offices. Consider if you could bring in and maximize the contributions of external contract talent when you encountered workload peaks or encountered a skills gap. Consider if you could repurpose your senior staff from current and unclear roles into a specific, high-value role of talent development or project execution.

In our digital economy, organizational success in the coming decades will depend on global talent and effective remote tech teams. With video conferencing and collaboration tools, we no longer need to be sitting in corporate headquarters. With digital learning, anyone with the drive to do the self-improvement can excel. While universities are indispensable, talent is available who may not have attended school in Boston or San Francisco. University is no longer the sole determination of competency.

### 6.3.2 Organizational Strategy and Global Talent Pools

Many (not all) traditional managers dislike contractors or external services because of a lack of control. Let's unpack what *control* means (see Table 6.2).

### Table 6.2 Output vs. Outcome

| Output-focused management—invented for the factory world | Outcome-focused management—required for a digital world |
|---|---|
| Micromanagers—manager tells employees what to do | Team lead sets clear team outcomes |
| Creates employee–employee competition, fine for one individual per task | Creates employee–employee collaboration, good for tech teams working toward some common objective |

## 6.4 The Evolving Organization and Functional Managers

### 6.4.1 For Tech, Functional Managers Evolve to Program Managers or Skills Development

In the effective remote organizations proposed, all managers evolve to program managers and GMs (Microsoft is pioneering here) *or* evolve to training and skills development. With self-managing teams guided by stated outcomes, there is no longer a need for functional management, and this change can be hard on organizations and people. Also, for the digital economy, this change is mandatory, based on industry evidence of businesses who thrive and businesses who fail to survive.

Top-down management, for tech, is nearing extinction. Management is evolving past *defensive* "inward facing" micromanagement focused on reducing costs and evolving to *offensive* "outward facing" customer-facing/market facing, data-driven market analytics and measurable outcomes.

The role of top executives/GMs/product line managers/program managers is understanding the market, identifying underserved markets, defining the measurable outcomes to service underserved markets. They direct/support/fund teams to solve tech problems and accomplish the desired outcomes.

Going forward, top executives/GMs/product line managers will focus outward on customers and customer pain, on outcomes and spending, less on managing individuals.

Increasingly, digital economies are based in data science, artificial intelligence, and machine learning because these are capable of tackling complex business problems with statistics to improve operations and retain and expand customers. WalMart® grew to the largest business on the planet by "simply" matching the right product to the right customer. OK, not exactly "simple" at Walmart's scale of thousands of stores selling millions of unique products to millions of unique customers while optimizing pricing, and seasonality, and logistics. More on data science to come.

## 6.4.2 The Evolving Organization and HR

When hiring (program managers and senior/executive people), look for serial successes (see Table 6.3). It's reasonable to make candidates defend their body of work, and we should do more of that. What projects were business successes? How much was spent, and how much was earned? Good executives will know the answer. If not, it's likely they aren't good executives. Hire on successes, don't hire based on previous title. Don't hire serial failures.

**Table 6.3 Evolving HR**

| Less of This | More of This |
|---|---|
| We need a VP, recruit someone who was a VP. | We need a great VP, let's look first for an internal promotion. |
| HR, look at title, pay, degree, nothing more. | HR, look at candidate body of work and successes. |
| Let's find the person with the best title and the lowest price tag (not look at success or body of work). | Many VP candidates are serial failures. These VPs wouldn't be available if they were serial successes, right? |

Don't hire jerks. Look at someone who has solid, positive 360° feedback from peers and subordinates. If they've managed big organizations, get insights about attrition, interview people who left.

## 6.4.3 HR and Outcome-Based Workplaces

- **Real-life experience** (✎): I once joined a team as product manager. The team included sales, ops manager, and tech marketing manager. We were together responsible for a product line of computer hardware components. Everyone on the team had a quarterly bonus based on a shared quarterly objective: achieve $X gross margin dollars for the coming quarter. At the start of each quarter, we got together and went through the possibilities of how to exceed our $GM target. We agreed on a short list of things we would do together as well as our individual responsibilities.

  The key learning was that our common goals motivated us to work together, and work together we did. For 11 quarters out of 12, we exceeded target, and we were all compensated above bonus target, remarkably without drama.

- **Real-life experience** (☝): This was at a large tech company which used the ranking+rating system. Every year various functional managers would gather in a conference room and rank some employee pool of similar function and seniority.

The key learning was: people in the same rank pool *would do things to improve their ranking, usually at the expense of others* in the same rank pool. Claiming undeserved credit, placing undeserved blame, and dysfunctional projects were the norm. It got worse: managers who did the ranking would give favorable assignments to their favorites and crappy assignments to those on their team they didn't like. This led to a culture in which no one offered constructive criticism. The drama was over the top. For me (and many others), it was a profoundly bad place to work.

- **Real-life experience** (👍): I worked for a tech company with a rigid twice-software release schedule. Our team was tasked with a death march: port a piece of complex code to a different type of Unix on a fixed schedule. The team lead found a modest budget (something less than $10,000), and, at the beginning of the project, wrote each team member a letter—at the beginning of the project, in writing—stating that a modest cash bonus ($500–$1000) would be available for achieving the port on schedule.

The key learning was that the bonus was offered beforehand, for specific results; everyone had the same incentive and the same specific results. There was near zero drama, and the goals were achieved. This was a good place to work.

---

**GOOD PRACTICES**

»  Shared goals matter more for remote teams.
»  Clearly stated results tied to a shared reward which is known at the start.

## 6.4.4 Reviews

Individual performance review. Really? Stop that! Reviews take people to their failures. Why not take people to their successes (appreciative recognition)?

Ranking+rating. Stop that too! It's not healthy, doesn't encourage team work, doesn't encourage good management. We need fewer individual performance reviews, and any sort of ranking+rating is not helpful. In my experience ranking+rating only perpetuates toxic behavior from managers and teammates.

We need less stick and more carrot. Our objective is not to dispense punishment, but to reward positive behaviors, improve results, and, wherever possible, reduce negative employment experiences. We need less attendance tracking, sick day tracking, vacation tracking, and the like. We need market value and results.

### 6.4.5 Compensation and HR Reviews—Team Goals and Results-Based Incentives

Team leaders need help from functional managers. If resources are getting peeled off for some other purpose, tell the team leader. If performance appraisal or feedback doesn't include project work and 360° project feedback, tell the team leader.

It is helpful to evaluate on-the-job and market value; just execution, everything has a goal, some sort of success criteria.

### 6.4.6 But What About Those Who Abuse "Work from Anywhere"?

The short answer, measure results (period). In our era of code, content, and causality, old school management just doesn't work. Management wants control. They want people to punch a clock, equating punctuality with production.

You may assume employees require constant oversight. But our recent experiences with quarantine have shown that employees are generally more productive. Yes, there will be some poor behavior, and team leads are well positioned to deal with that; just give team lead the authority.

*Attendance punctuality is truly irrelevant.* We have all witnessed people who arrive early, leave late, and contribute little. We have all witnessed people who keep unusual hours and deliver exceptional results. Results matter.

*Meeting punctuality matters* when we are interacting with the team. Missing or being tardy for calls impacts collaboration and team progress. It is reasonable to place importance on call attendance and punctuality.

No one is suggesting we drop all accountability. Rather, we suggest that accountability be evolved to simply show market value and results. Does anything else really matter?

- HR knows salary bands and bonuses for various skill/experience levels, so that's a starting point.
- Team lead knows/tracks results.
- Team 360° feedback from peers and subordinates is necessary. Yes, the subordinates should objectively rate their functional managers and team leads (no toxicity allowed).

The focus is team incentives and team success criteria—scope, schedule, resource, risk, revenue, margin. This works, I have experienced it firsthand.

360° feedback helps identify and correct toxic functional managers and team leads.

Set teams up to help each other achieve results and reward that behavior.

### 6.4.7 HR and Organizational Appetite for Innovation

It is HR's job get the best possible value from employees on behalf of the organization. Fear is counterproductive for any organization attempting to innovate. We fear making mistakes; we fear being wrong. And our fears are magnified when our livelihoods are at risk in individual HR performance evaluations or interacting with overzealous functional management. Perceived risks of being wrong create real headwinds to innovation.

First, we can unpack the root causes of fear and then take steps to overcome those fears to increase innovation. Fear is a primitive emotion. Our primitive instincts cause us to fear the risk of being wrong or risk of social ostracism. This is how all of us are wired, and our primitive fear of risk and fear of the unknown will not disappear simply because they are inconvenient.

Especially in tech, we fear being wrong, and this inhibits our motivation to innovate. There are so many things that can go wrong, resulting in rejection and embarrassment. It triggers our primal fear of being ostracized.

When team contributors perceive that they will be negatively judged if they are wrong, they will just wait to be told what to do, and if it fails, they are not to blame. Accordingly, there are no attempts at anything new, and zero innovation ensues. This fear of being less than perfect often results in procrastination. Behaviors of risk avoidance, reluctance to make a decision, waiting to be told what to do, procrastination, inability to stay on task, and excessive demands for details of assigned tasks are all signals of an unhealthy work environment.

To overcome our primitive instinct, we must take conscious actions to create a workplace that embraces the inevitable mistakes that come with innovation. Specifically, self-directed teams (without interference of functional managers and without counterproductive individual performance focus) are the basis of workplaces which foster innovation. Self-directed teams can process mistakes in a healthy way:

- Our goals, user feedback, and user stories suggest we try this innovation.
- We tried that innovation, and we learned it did not work, and we learned why.
- From those lessons we tried some other innovation; this attempt worked better.

Notice, upper management still establishes key success factors and measurable outcomes. This establishes a safe space in which mistakes are OK and innovation can occur.

Our primitive brains yell at us, "Don't take the risk, don't risk being wrong." This line of thinking is negative and defensive. Our counter balance to this primitive brain function is to use our frontal cortex to know the consequences of doing nothing. This is an important conversation to have with the team, and it's important to revisit the "consequences of doing nothing" topic often. User feedback, user stories are a strong motivator. User stories paint a clear picture of success and reduce the perceived risk of being wrong.

Our big picture moment . . . all companies participate in the digital economy, all companies are tech companies. When we discuss effective remote tech teams, these are the capabilities, core skills, and the building blocks of successful companies.

Google Cloud CEO Thomas Kurian, in his concluding remarks to a major keynote presentation mid-2020, said this[3]:

> *This is a very defining moment for all of us around the world—to have the hope and the optimism to reimagine your business as you recover from the pandemic.*

## 6.5 Remote Teams and Ongoing Professional Development

Employee satisfaction (in large part) is driven by a need to achieve mastery.

Google® offers a "spend part of your week innovating" workshop. Yes, it is supervised, it's not just play time. This is relevant, as it gives the employee an avenue to achieve mastery, to invent, to create. This leads to contributions back to the organization, new research, content on thought leadership, new code, new patents, happier employees, and lower turnover.

For your teams, individuals will appreciate professional development. It should be supervised, and it's appropriate to have the individual brief the team on the professional development they've done and what they got out of it.

Everyone on the team should do professional development. When you bump into teammates who don't engage, nudge them on a one-to-one call. It's important they hear confirmation that they are important, and they hear the company is investing in their growth. The "call to action" is for them to see it as an opportunity, and it's useful for the teammate to contribute their best back to the team (make it about the team).

Another essential professional development message is that we recognize it will not be easy every step of the way, there will be difficulties, there will be setbacks, but we are all pulling on the same end of the rope—we succeed together.

The underlying reasons: contribute to the team, invest the time, and report out. There is nothing like teaching a topic to fully understand it.

---

[3] https://cloudwars.co/google-cloud/google-cloud-next-thomas-kurians-vision-fastest -growing-cloud/

## 6.6 Static Mindset and Growth Mindset

Too many companies' cultures reward avoiding failure rather than achieving results and success. This is the culture of static thinking. The culture of growth thinking rewards values, achievement, and results.

Static thinking: "Things are what they are, they won't change."

Growth thinking: "Change takes effort, and change takes time, but things will change."

We are wired to hunger for growth, to explore, to learn, to gain wisdom. Regrettably, some have allowed themselves to become convinced that nothing will change, that problems are caused by others, and the system is weighted against our success by "them." Those choosing employment by these static organizational cultures are making a conscious choice of compensation versus a rewarding career. Increasingly, organizations can offer both compensation *and* a rewarding career, and so corporate evolution, survival of the fittest, comes into play. Growth-thinking companies attract the talent, grow, and thrive, while static thinking companies lose talent, shrink, and die.

We know that organizations cannot afford to take on every idea, and it's important to temper expectations, but you can make a conscious choice to have a static mindset or a growth mindset, and it will be reflected by your team.

*The mistake of the "not invented here" mindset.* Another example of static mindsets are evident in beliefs that all tech and all intellectual property (IP) must be internally generated and that reliance on anything created by others poses an unacceptable risk. Counter to this thinking, why re-invent what is already available and do the ongoing maintenance and the ongoing security analysis? Why not just crowdsource that so internal talent is available for innovative and highly relevant tasks?

### 6.6.1 Resourcefulness

We live in an imperfect world of finite budgets but near-infinite needs. We will constantly encounter situations in which we don't have enough time, the right skills, or the right resources to overcome some significant problem or significant risk.

If you are with a technical product/services company, "non-recoverable engineering (NRE) funds" is a negative term for the technical team, as they assume they are on a short leash and at the mercy of those providing the funds. Their value is temporary.

True story: A software business development exec from an open-source software company negotiated a significant NRE deal ($50M+) with a major silicon company. This project involved a substantial statement of work and an 18-month timeline. This is nothing new, it happens all the time. What happens next, is *not* typical.

The software company started to execute on the NRE project and made reasonable progress (established credibility), and during a normal quarterly meeting their business development exec proposed a significant adjustment to the statement of work, and he sold it well. The silicon company agreed.

The result was that the statement of work was adjusted to align to the software company roadmap. The software company's business development exec was successful in having the silicon company fund work that the software company was going to do anyway and fund themselves. Resourcefulness.

The essence of this moment was an alignment of goals between the silicon company and the software company.

This is relevant for teams, as the answer is not always "build it ourselves, we are engineers, we build stuff, that's our job, not someone else's job." The counterbalance to this mindset (often encountered) is that not every task is high value. It's OK to have others do lower-value tasks, because that frees up our team to do higher-value tasks. Make it about setting the team up for success and contributing value to your organization.

## 6.7 Company-Level Remote Teams, a Competitive Advantage

Remote teams are such a necessity that they deserve executive attention. There are organizations that have a standing executive committee to oversee and improve distributed teams.

Following is an outline for a remote teams handbook:

- Write down guidelines and examples for projects, processes, sales, collateral. Clear, simple docs, not watercoolers.
- Meetings: have an agenda, record all meetings, have a wiki.
- Guidelines on dedicating workspace, work/life balance, mental health, exercise, sleep (say it's OK, say it's advisable).
- Common remote tools for teams internally and for teams to use with outside folks.
- Common tools to share files, track POR, track results.
- Report results, both the good and not good; embrace iteration.
- Reward contribution, reward results.
- Conduct 360° reviews, include subordinates and other organizations, and listen.

Hire the best talent available, regardless of location. Measure results, avoid measuring irrelevant stuff. Do "all hands." Be clear about company values, make the connection.

### 6.7.1 Access to a Global Talent Pool

Frequently overlooked is the access to a global talent pool. Global talent (often incorrectly referred to as "outsourcing") is either a competitive disadvantage or a competitive advantage. Companies that fail to take advantage of global talent are disadvantaged. Global talent is a huge advantage if that talent can be meaningfully applied and produce results.

### 6.7.2 Why Outsourcing or Offshoring Has a Bad Rep and How to Fix It

The short answer: leadership did a bad job of it. Tech outsourcing over the last decade was mostly a failure. That's a big claim, but successful, high-ROI outsourcing case studies are few.

We recognize that prior attempts to off-shore were driven by efforts to cut costs and were mostly focused on uncool work in low-value functional areas. People do not choose to study software for the opportunity to do patch testing or related drudge work. People in these jobs are typically low-job-satisfaction people. Typically, offshore people are not rewarded for innovation or performance. They are most often just punished for mistakes. So, these talented and affordable people focus on avoiding mistakes, not producing anything of high value or anything innovative.

These low-value functional areas such as tech support, internationalization, testing, porting, and patching were typically thrown over the wall at remote services staff with near-zero care. These remote teams were poorly on-boarded, endured poor knowledge exchange, usually had no clear goals, no key success criteria, insufficient communication, and zero teamwork. Is anyone surprised that the root cause of these frequent failures is poor leadership?

Regrettably, some companies still reject the concept of outsourcing or contractors. In my opinion, these companies' policies cause them to be uncompetitive. A closer look will likely reveal a culture of control rather than a culture of results and merit.

The remedy to these chronic failures are:

- Clear goals, clear success criteria
- Active communication, engagement as a single team, not them and us
- A work environment that avoids magnifying the surviving instinct
- A work environment that emphasizes the belonging and becoming instincts
- Rewarding innovation, such as automated unit testing
- Managing risk, fixing blockers, setting the team up for success, celebrating mistakes

- Working together with purpose and enthusiasm
- Recognizing the value is in cross-functional teamwork, not just functional areas and cost saving.

The ability to *effectively* use remote talent opens up a competitive advantage.

### 6.7.3  Our New Model for Global Talent

We can learn from the practice of IT. (See Figure 6.1). Over recent decades, IT got complex and expensive. This led typical IT to reduce spending. Staff was reduced to only what was needed to run the day-to-day baseline operations, and when these typical IT departments were handed some non-baseline tasks (for which they were no longer staffed), they used contracts to deliver.

For example, if a company acquired another company, that's non-baseline. It is typical that outside contractors will be applied to adjust network domains, adjust security domains, add or subtract users from those security domains, adjust data storage, and migrate email.

Another example: A company that wants to consolidate or re-configure data centers, design/deploy new hardware, new network, new cloud, test/migration/monitoring. When Randy Mott took over the CIO position for Hewlett Packard®, he and his team consolidated 120+ HP data centers into 19 data centers. Datacenter migration is a very real example of non-baseline tasks.

The theme is: have permanent staff to manage baseline tasks, and have contractors (companies or individuals) to handle the non-baseline tasks. *Effective* remote teams are the key enabler of this baseline–non-baseline approach. *Effective* remote teams are the competitive advantage over those who are weak at executing with global talent.

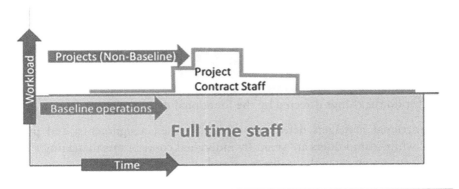

**Figure 6.1**   The New Model for Global Talent

The world now has an estimated 25 million software developers of all skills and price tags. Increasingly, we see highly experienced technologists with very specific skills available and affordable. These developers can be a competitive advantage to your company—or they can be a competitive advantage of your competition. This theme also includes digital marketing, designers, trainers, content creators, sales, and many other transferrable skills. These highly skilled and highly experienced specialists are typically available for less money than one would pay an early- or mid-career technologist with generalist skills.

If you have a choice of spending money on tech talent within commuting distance of your offices, very possibly in the bay area, Boston, Tokyo, or other high-cost-of-living locale, versus spending the same or less money on a specialist with direct experience, what sane person would not choose the latter?

Throwing people and money at a task does not guarantee success. Winners in the coming decades will be those who *effectively* use the global talent pool. Leadership avoids surviving instincts and excites belonging and becoming instincts. Leadership delivers results.

### 6.7.4 Empowered Team Leads

Early in my career, I became aware that the majority of tech projects fail. I concluded that if someone—a project manager, team leader, program manager—could drive project success, the project manager function would be a highly valued career path.

I was wrong.

I wrongly assumed that project managers (PMs) have the authority to go along with the responsibility. There is an obvious blocker. For the PM to have control, the functional managers must give up control. This erodes the career value of the functional manager. These headwinds are faced by every company. Either leave the control in the hands of functional managers (and continue to see failed projects), or place control in the hands of the PM over the objections and passive resistance of the functional managers.

This leaves individual contributors with conflicting directives:

- Do the things directed by the team lead.
- Or do the things directed by the functional department managers.

Functional managers determine raises, bonuses, assignments, and promotions, while team leaders are typically individual contributors managing a cross-functional resources without direct control.

"Good actor" functional managers will coordinate with the team lead with relevant task assignments relating to the project.

"Bad actor" functional managers (regrettably too numerous) will "grab for the wheel" and redirect people, micromanage, change priorities, or add side projects on a whim.

However, there is no need to vilify functional leaders as they develop core competencies. Companies who choose to adopt a PM-led culture must have good-actor functional leaders who are willing and able to work with PMs. To turn the corner from functional focused to cross-functional team focused, it may be necessary to self-benchmark your own company successes *with* cross-functional leadership to your successes *without* cross-functional leadership. Also, it's advisable to benchmark your company success rates against other companies' success rates.

Integrated product teams are the core of Microsoft's success. They combine product management, project management, development, sales, marketing, and user interface design. The good news is that, based on Microsoft (and other successes), the PM company culture is increasing in success rates.

Global talent pools require high-quality team leadership. When an organization says, "We don't outsource. We don't use contractors," the inevitable failure's root cause is poor management, not poor talent. And that points to a functional organization built around silos, rather than a cross-functional organization built around results.

I have worked in multiple large organizations with a functional focus rather than a cross-functional team focus. These functional-focused companies rarely have decent PMs, and therefore they rarely use global talent pools. My educated guess is that, without good PMs, efforts with global talent fail as a result of poor on-boarding, lack of communication, and lack of collaboration.

The choice is simple: companies can stick with functional leadership, and the ongoing outcomes (most often failure); *or* companies can focus on team/PM leadership, focus on results, outcomes, and key success criteria shared by cross-functional teams.

## 6.8 Trail Map and Conclusion

In the digital era, I firmly believe, the only sane approach to management is cross-functional teams, with clarity on customer-relevant problems to solve and measurable outcomes.

But what about those who abuse work from anywhere? The short answer: measure results (period).

The contrast between management by outcomes and management by controls (outputs) is stark. Management by controls, such as in factories, count items, quality, hours, etc. In the digital era, are we counting lines of code, code defects? This is ineffective and ridiculous. Management by controls fails in the digital era.

Successful, effective project team results are measured by key success criteria. In the absence of clear project success criteria, concerns that remote people will slack are real. But when projects are properly conceived, well run, with clear and measurable goals, those thin and misguided objections are demonstrably misguided. Those arguing that people are lazy and remote people don't work cling to a false belief that old-school controls/output-based management work for the digital era. They conveniently ignore inconsistent project execution, high permanent headcount, excessive spending on office space, and a digital talent pool limited to commuting distance of their offices.

Use the remote teams maturity model (see page 99) to set goals and measure progress. Effective remote teams are going to take a minute. Measure progress. You can expect resistance, typically from HR and functional managers who like their kingdoms. Some of those functional managers will successfully transition to team leads, others will not. Leaving control in the hands of functional management and HR is unhealthy.

When you do *real teams,* where the team leads have real authority to accompany accountability, the result will be a highly competitive organization with a sure-footed project execution. The result will be a more innovative organization focused on customer-relevant problems, reduced permanent headcount, lower payroll, higher employee satisfaction. Spending will be reduced for permanent office space, energy, insurance, and security.

*The most significant change is the global talent pool to recruit from.*

# Chapter 7

# Closing Thoughts

This book was written in the Spring/Summer of 2020, during the pandemic, at a time when, wherever possible, we stayed home. The resulting world-wide experience showed that work from home is practical for those companies that already embrace the principles of effective remote tech teams. Work from home (or work from anywhere) is our new normal. The only open question is which companies will survive and thrive and which companies will struggle.

We submit, organizations with "work from anywhere" augmented with *effective* remote teams and a global talent pool will thrive. And organizations insisting on a rigid "in-the-office" policy will struggle to reduce attrition, attract talent, and afford talent.

## 7.1 Remote Work: Spend Less, Do More

One-hundred percent remote is becoming the new norm for software development organizations. One-hundred-percent-remote organizations can recruit candidates from any location, and the available talent pool is incredibly expanded. There are lower facilities expenses and a bigger talent pool to recruit from at a lower payroll burden.

Here is the ROI for required attendance:

- Micromanagement is more possible and typically the norm.
- Increased spending on office space, furniture, office equipment such as printers, badges, networks, landlines, power, cleaning.

- Increased spending on security and property insurance.
- A talent pool limited to candidates within commute range.
- Relocation expenses.
- Reduced attendance for those with significant commutes.

In contrast, here is the ROI for remote:

- Significantly lower spending on office space, furniture, cleaning, security, etc.
- Reduced spending on power.
- Significantly expanded talent pool.
- Higher productivity, lower attrition, loyalty.

Multiple surveys consistently report compelling benefits.[1] Improvements cited by employees surveyed in the studies:

- Better work–life balance (91%)
- Increased productivity/better focus (79%)
- Less stress (78%)
- Avoid a commute (78%)
- Several part-time employees splitting one job

Remote work, yes, we will spend less and do more. Remote work can be set up as partially remote, partially in the office, but increasingly is set up as 100% remote, using video conferencing and other collaboration tools to take full advantage of global talent pools.

## 7.2 Effective Remote Tech Teams Core Competency

Organizational core competency requires conscious efforts to eliminate the invisible "us-versus-them" barriers. Permanent employees must be actively coached to treat contract/temporary employees as equals.

And likewise, contract/temporary employees must be actively coached to be assertive and contribute just as other full-time employees do. Recognize the similar invisible barriers for contributors whose first language is not English. Recognize the invisible barriers for those who are either naturally or culturally passive and expect to be told what to do, rather than be assertive or take initiative. These are learned working styles and may not be natural for everyone on

---

[1]   https://www.inc.com/brit-morse/remote-work-survey-owl-labs.html;
   https://www.citrix.com/content/dam/citrix/en_us/documents/white-paper/economic
   -impacts-flexible-working-us-2019.pdf

the team. Active inclusion results in everyone contributing to the shared goals of the team to contribute their best.

## 7.3 Teambuilding Exercises

Work can be a little fun—it's allowed. Team building helps us to feel like we fit in. It speaks directly to our wiring to be part of the tribe, part of the society.

### 7.3.1 Team Building Exercise—The Wilson Gambit, Storytelling (Done on Group Video)

Each person takes a turn telling the class a story. Each story should take two minutes to tell, with emphasis on communicating some key message.

After all participants have their turns, the group votes on the most meaningful, best overall, best humor, and largest impact. Leader sums up with why story matters in teams (both within the team and beyond the immediate team.)

### 7.3.2 Team Building Exercise—How to Provide Constructive and Healthy Feedback

This exercise is to demonstrate how to give and receive help.

Make up situations, role play, put the team lead in a junior position, put junior people in senior positions, group critique (go around the table, things to do more of, things to do less of).

Find empathy:

- Offer help without being arrogant, receive help without being defensive.
- Replay the problem statement. Think outside the box on the solution.
- "I like working with you."

### 7.3.3 Team Building Exercise—Wichita Lineman

- Ben writes a line.
- Beth writes a line, throws Ben a curveball.
- Ben writes the next line, throws Beth a curveball.
- And so on until we get to a conclusion. Drive it like you stole it.

The benefit is that this lets loose a bit of creativity with team members, but outside of a formal team setting. Plus, it's pretty fun.

### 7.3.4 Team Building Exercise—The Agile Penny Game

This little game helps agile software teams better understand and embrace focus on a short list of small and manageable chunks of work rather than big chunks or big lists.

Start with 20 pennies.

**Iteration 1: Developers—Bill, Audrey, Danny, Eddie—batch size 20**

- Place all 20 pennies heads up in front of Bill.
- Start the timer.
- Bill must flip over all 20 pennies, then pass all 20 pennies to the left to Audrey.
- Audrey must flip all 20 pennies and pass to Danny.
- Danny must flip all 20 pennies and pass to Eddie.
- Eddie must flip all 20 pennies and pass to Bill.
- Stop the timer when all pennies are returned to Bill.

**Iteration 2: Developers—Bill, Audrey, Danny, Eddie—batch size 10**

- Place two batches of 10 pennies each, heads up in front of Bill.
- Start the timer.
- Bill flips over batch 10 pennies, then passes to Audrey. Bill flips over the next batch of 10 pennies, passes to Audrey.
- Audrey starts on first batch, passes to Danny, then starts on next batch, passes to Danny.
- Danny starts on first batch, passes to Eddie, then starts on next batch, passes to Bill.
- Eddie starts on first batch, passes to Bill, then starts on next batch, passes to Bill.
- Stop timer when all pennies are returned to Bill.

**Iteration 3: Developers—Bill, Audrey, Danny, Eddie—batch size 5**

- Place four batches of five pennies each, heads up in front of Bill.
- Start the timer.
- Bill flips over batch five pennies, then passes to Audrey. Bill flips over the next batch of five pennies and passes to Audrey.
- You get the idea.
- Stop timer when all pennies are returned to Bill.

The takeaway: A tight team collaborating on a tight list of small jobs gets more done in less time. See Table 7.1.

Table 7.1 Agile Penny Game Results

|  | Iteration 1 | Iteration 2 | Iteration 3 |
|---|---|---|---|
| Number of coins | 20 | 20 | 20 |
| Coins per batch | 20 | 10 | 5 |
| Time to complete | 54 seconds | 43 seconds | 35 seconds |

# 7.4 My Statement on Meritocracy vs. Racism and Other Discrimination

We are wired for racism. Snap judgment: 80,000 years ago it was a matter of survival, it is the stuff our gene pool is made of. The problem is we are now in a modern workplace, and 4,000 generations of wiring hasn't caught up. *Not us or one of us.*

- Predator or prey
- Danger or safety

Regrettably, we are wired for racism. Snap judgments, us versus them, prejudice. BUT THIS DOES NOT EXCUSE RACISM.

I believe silence = acceptance. I will not be silent; I will do all I can to correct racial prejudice and make the world a little bit better place.

I DO NOT ACCEPT RACISM.

How to remedy? It takes conscious effort to counterbalance the instinct to snap judgment, which puts our decision process off balance. In the absence of conscious effort, our snap judgments will give the nod to people who look like us, regardless of merit. Obviously, these effect hiring decisions, but also day-to-day stuff, like who gets the choice tasks and who gets the crummy tasks, who gets heard and who doesn't, who gets promotions/raises/bonuses and who doesn't.

I tick all the wrong boxes—White, male, Southerner, not born into poverty, born in America. I cannot change the circumstances of my birth or race. I cannot fully know what it is like to live every hour of every day as Black male in a country which still embraces institutionalized racism.

We know Black parents tell their children, "Being just as good as your White classmate is not good enough, you need to be significantly better, you need to work significantly harder than others." I cannot imagine having *that* conversation with *my* 12-year-old child, but Black parents must. No doubt other minorities have the same conversation. For generations, they have had to work significantly harder to earn equal pay and equal opportunity for advancement, and often even that fell short.

I cannot change my race or gender or sexual preference, any more than others can. But what I *can* do (what *we* can do), is follow the example above. I (we) can be significantly better at consciously counterbalancing our wiring.

We need to work harder to consciously create a meritocracy in which results, quality, care, teamwork, helping others, and outcomes are rewarded, regardless of everything else. While this conversation has mostly cited Blacks, it is equally true of women and other minorities—anyone who doesn't look like us, who doesn't pray like us, who doesn't love like us; we make a *conscious* effort to make it a meritocracy for them.

A closing note: I have had countless people of color go out of their way to do something kind and noble for me, without anything for them to personally gain. I am a better person for these many moments in my limited time on earth.

# 7.5 Trail Map and Conclusion

## Playbook for Effective Remote Tech Teams

| |
|---|
| PHASE 1: Define a modest project; this is a trial of effective remote teams' methods in your organization. This is your learning project. Make it cross-function, make it important but without significant business risk if problems arise. |
| Have everyone read this book. |
| Define the goals and outcome. |
| Define the power metrics—measured by customer usage, customer satisfaction, or similar. Avoid changing goals and metrics, stability makes this work. |
| Well-stated project goals—paint a clear definition of success, share with the team early and often. |
| Cross-functional contributions (so the power metrics are within the teams' abilities). |
| Involve engineering, ops, helpdesk, marketing, sales, HR; cross-functional participants with common/shared cross functional goals make this work. |
| Assign an executive sponsor who will brief the functional leads involved; interrupt resources only in emergencies, and only after alerting team lead. |
| Establish a wiki (or similar) to clarify plan of record, agendas, action tracking. |
| Clarify devops using same wiki—where to sandbox, test, deploy. |
| Code reviews, build/version schedules, automate testing, defect logging. |
| Capture non-tech in same wiki—presentations, sales training, support knowledge exchange. |
| Assign a team lead and contributors, ideally remote (obviously) and with external resources. |
| Write the project plan as a problem statement; engineers love problems as they give room to create and expand. Avoid dictating solutions. |

| |
|---|
| Involve HR to conduct simple job satisfaction surveys at beginning, early, middle, late, and end of project.<br><br>Overall, how is your job satisfaction?<br><br>Is working remote improving or diminishing your productivity?<br><br>How is the collaboration and teams abilities to innovate and solve problems together?<br><br>Are you comfortable with team goals rather than individual goals?<br><br>Is working remotely improving or diminishing your work/life balance?<br><br>Do you feel your contribution to the team is improving or diminishing?<br><br>Do you feel your contribution to the organization is improving or diminishing?<br><br>Is your understanding of the usefulness of project to our busines improving or diminishing?<br><br>Look for HR survey changes over time as the project progresses from beginning to middle to end. |
| Team leader + contributor one-to-one meetings early and often. Are you set up for success? Do you have what you need (including external contributors, especially external contributors)? |
| Do team calls often. Use inclusive meeting protocols.<br><br>Agendas will engage others to present (most meetings will not be dominated by team lead).<br><br>Ask the team if they are encountering blockers.<br><br>Ask each individual, by name, if they'd like to share anything with the team. Do this consistently, and the group will relax and speak up. |
| Collect weekly status reports: 0%, 25%, 50%, 75%, and done.<br><br>Set a deadline (say noon Friday), and pick up the phone at 1 PM if you haven't received. It may take a couple of times, but soon enough phone calls will not be needed. |
| Manage risk, discuss risk with the team early and often. |
| Manage the scope of work—execution of version 1.0 is the top priority.<br><br>Build a roadmap, and requests for changes land in version 2, version 3. |
| Team lead will brief leadership frequently; transparency is good: scope, schedule, resources, quality. |
| Team lead reports bad news. Contributors report good news. No exceptions. |

# Appendix

## A.1  Diagram and Roles of Our Brains[1]

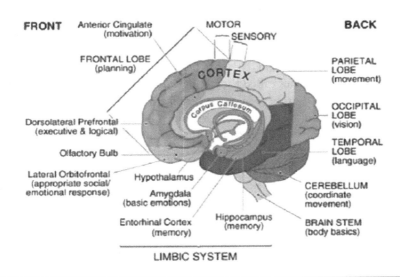

**Figure A.1**  The Human Brain (*Source:* brainwaves.com, used with permission)

---

[1]  The definitions and diagrams are from Brainwaves.com, used with permission.

- **Amygdala:** Lying deep in the center of the limbic emotional brain, this powerful structure, the size and shape of an almond, is constantly alert to the needs of basic survival, including sex, emotional reactions such as anger and fear. Consequently, it inspires aversive cues, such as sweaty palms, and has recently been associated with a range of mental conditions including depression to even autism. It is larger in male brains, often enlarged in the brains of sociopaths, and it shrinks in the elderly.

**Brain Stem:** The part of the brain that connects to the spinal cord. The brain stem controls functions basic to the survival of all animals, such as heart rate, breathing, digesting foods, and sleeping. It is the lowest, most primitive area of the human brain. [Often referred to as the "lizard brain."]

- **Cerebellum:** Two peach-size mounds of folded tissue located at the top of the brain stem, the cerebellum is the guru of skilled, coordinated movement (e.g., returning a tennis serve or throwing a slider down and in) and is involved in some learning pathways.
- **Cerebrum:** This is the largest brain structure in humans and accounts for about two-thirds of the brain's mass. It is divided into two sides—the left and right hemispheres—that are separated by a deep groove down the center from the back of the brain to the forehead. These two halves are connected by long neuron branches called the *corpus callosum*, which is relatively larger in women's brains than in men's. The cerebrum is positioned over and around most other brain structures, and its four lobes are specialized by function but are richly connected. The outer three millimeters of "gray matter" is the cerebral cortex, which consists of closely packed neurons that control most of our bodily functions, including the mysterious state of consciousness, the senses, the body's motor skills, reasoning and language.
  - The *Frontal Lobe* is the most recently evolved part of the brain and the last to develop in young adulthood. Its dorso-lateral prefrontal circuit is the brain's top executive. It organizes responses to complex problems, plans steps to an objective, searches memory for relevant experience, adapts strategies to accommodate new data, guides behavior with verbal skills, and houses working memory. Its orbitofrontal circuit manages emotional impulses in socially appropriate ways for productive behaviors including empathy, altruism, interpretation of facial expressions. Stroke in this area typically releases foul language and fatuous behavior patterns.
  - The *Temporal Lobe* controls memory storage area, emotion, hearing, and, on the left side, language.
  - The *Parietal Lobe* receives and processes sensory information from the body, including calculating location and speed of objects.

○ The *Occipital Lobe* processes visual data and routes it to other parts of the brain for identification and storage.

**Hippocampus:** Located deep within the brain, it processes new memories for long-term storage. If you didn't have it, you couldn't live in the present; you'd be stuck in the past of old memories. It is among the first functions to falter in Alzheimer's.

**Hypothalamus:** Located at the base of the brain where signals from the brain and the body's hormonal system interact, the hypothalamus maintains the body's status quo. It monitors numerous bodily functions such as blood pressure and body temperature, as well as controlling body weight and appetite.

**Thalamus:** Located at the top of the brain stem, the thalamus acts as a two-way relay station, sorting, processing, and directing signals from the spinal cord and mid-brain structures up to the cerebrum, and, conversely, from the cerebrum down the spinal cord to the nervous system.

## A.2  Our Evolutionary Timeline

- Six million years ago: Humans evolved from our most recent ancestor (common with chimpanzees), estimated as 300,000 generations.
- Fifty thousand years ago: We began to act as communal groups with primitive communications based on gestures, sounds, and facial expressions.
- Ten thousand years ago: Agrarian society started. Counting, trade, and money appeared [*imagine a world without money*].
- Five hundred years ago: Literacy became widespread.
- Two hundred years ago: The first industrial age (factories, steam, rail, and electric power).
- Less than one hundred years ago: The second industrial age (electronics, radio, aircraft).
- Less than fifty years ago: The third industrial age (digital communications, computers, internet, databases, email).
- Less than ten years ago: The fourth industrial age (augmented intelligence, machine learning, artificial intelligence).
- This year: The first pandemic in the Internet age. Driving social distancing and work from home.

Too few generations for evolution. Our environment is changing orders of magnitude faster than our brains can evolve. As leaders, we can compensate. See Figure A.2.

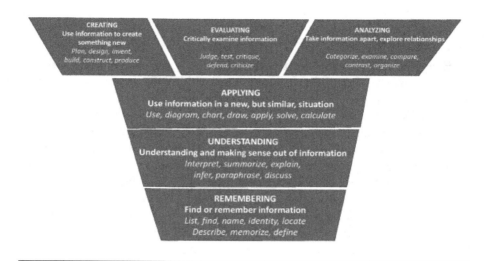

**Figure A.2**   Blooms Hierarchy of Learning

# Index

Printed in the United States
by Baker & Taylor Publisher Services